SIGMUND FREUD

IMMORTALS OF SCIENCE

SIGMUND
FREUD

by Francine Klagsbrun

Franklin Watts, Inc.
575 Lexington Avenue • *New York, N.Y.* *10022*

ACKNOWLEDGMENTS

Permission has been given to quote from the following publications in this work:

Sigmund Freud, *An Autobiographical Study*. W. W. Norton & Company, Inc., New York, 1952.

Sigmund Freud, *The Ego and the Id*. W. W. Norton & Company, Inc., New York, 1960.

Letters of Sigmund Freud, ed. by Ernst L. Freud. Basic Books, Inc., Publishers, New York, 1960. Hogarth Press, Ltd., London.

Sigmund Freud, *The Origins of Psycho-Analysis, Letters to Wilhelm Fliess, Drafts and Notes: 1887–1902*. Basic Books, Inc., Publishers, New York, 1954. Hogarth Press, Ltd., London, 1959.

Ernest Jones, *The Life and Work of Sigmund Freud*. 3 vols. Basic Books, Inc., Publishers, New York, 1953–57. Hogarth Press, Ltd., London, 1953–57.

Jung, Carl G. *Memories, Dreams, Reflections*. Random House, Inc., 1963.

Contents

Foreword

The greatness of Sigmund Freud lies not only in the ideas and techniques he discovered, but in his unusual ability to present those ideas and techniques clearly and excitingly. Freud was a master of prose writing, and by far the best explanations of even his most complicated theories are his own explanations.

Freud left an enormous number of writings. In addition to his many books, papers, and pamphlets, he composed thousands of letters to friends, family members, and even casual acquaintances. Many of these letters have been preserved and published in individual volumes. They provide deep insight into Freud's day-to-day thoughts and activities during his long life.

Much of the information in this biography is based on the writings and collections of letters by Freud listed below. Also helpful for background material were the source books about Freud by his contemporaries and followers included in the list.

WORKS BY FREUD

BREUER, JOSEPH AND FREUD, SIGMUND. *Studies in Hysteria.* Authorized tr. by A. A. Brill. Boston: Beacon Press, 1964.
FREUD, ERNST L. AND MENG, HEINRICH, EDS. *Psychoanalysis and*

Faith; Letters of Sigmund Freud and Oskar Pfister. Tr. by Eric Mosbacher. New York: Basic Books, Inc., Publishers, 1963.

FREUD, SIGMUND. *An Autobiographical Study.* Authorized tr. by James Strachey. New York: W. W. Norton & Company, Inc., 1952.

——. *The Basic Writings of Sigmund Freud.* Ed. by A. A. Brill. New York: Modern Library, Inc., 1938.

——. *Civilization and Its Discontents.* Authorized tr. by Joan Riviere. London: Hogarth Press, Ltd., 1930.

——. *Collected Papers.* 5 vols. Authorized tr. under the supervision of Joan Riviere. London: Hogarth Press, Ltd., 1953.

——. *The Ego and the Id.* Authorized tr. by Joan Riviere. New York: W. W. Norton & Company, Inc., 1960.

——. *A General Introduction to Psychoanalysis.* Authorized tr. by Joan Riviere. New York: Doubleday & Company, Inc., 1953.

——. *Letters of Sigmund Freud.* Ed. by Ernst L. Freud. Tr. by Tania and James Stern. New York: Basic Books, Inc., Publishers, 1960.

——. *Moses and Monotheism.* New York: Alfred A. Knopf, Inc., 1939.

——. *The Origins of Psycho-Analysis: Letters to Wilhelm Fleiss, Drafts and Notes, 1887–1902.* Ed. by M. Bonaparte and others. Authorized tr. by Eric Mosbacher and James Strachey. New York: Basic Books, Inc., Publishers, 1954.

——. *An Outline of Psychoanalysis.* Authorized tr. by James Strachey. London: Hogarth Press, Ltd., 1949.

WORKS ABOUT FREUD

BRILL, A. A. *Freud's Contribution to Psychiatry.* New York: W. W. Norton & Company, Inc., 1944.

BROWN, JAMES A. C. *Freud and the Post-Freudians.* London: Cassell & Co., Ltd. 1963.

DOOLITTLE, HILDA. *Tribute to Freud.* New York: Pantheon Books, Inc., 1956.

FREUD, MARTIN. *Sigmund Freud: Man and Father*. New York: Vanguard Press, Inc., 1958.

FROMM, ERICH. *Sigmund Freud's Mission*. New York: Grove Press, Inc., 1963.

JONES, ERNEST. *The Life and Work of Sigmund Freud*. 3 vols. New York: Basic Books, Inc., Publishers, 1953–1957.

JUNG, CARL G. *Memories, Dreams, Reflections*. Tr. by Richard and Clara Winston. New York: Random House, Inc., 1963.

REIK, THEODOR. *From Thirty Years with Freud*. New York: Farrar & Rinehart, Inc., 1940.

SACHS, HANNS. *Freud, Master and Friend*. Cambridge, Massachusetts: Harvard University Press, 1946.

STEKEL, WILHELM. *Autobiography of Wilhelm Stekel*. New York: Liveright Publishing Corp., 1950.

CHAPTER ONE

The Old Refugee

The old man moved slowly toward the platform. Pale and gaunt, but with head erect, he might have been a retired soldier or an aged statesman. Yet the look in his dark eyes, a look of sadness mixed with determination, spoke of something else. That special "something" about the man made the people around stop their talking and laughing to stare at him. Silently he boarded the train, and seated near a window, gazed long and hard at a land he would never see again.

Sigmund Freud was leaving Vienna, Austria—the city that had been his home for seventy-eight years. At the age of eighty-two, he was too old and sick, he told himself, to be making this trip. Yet he knew he had to go. That his life was at stake mattered little. What did matter was his lifetime's work, which must not die at the hands of the Nazi murderers. Sigmund Freud had devoted the long years of his life to unlocking the secrets of men's minds. His findings and his world-famous technique of psychoanalysis must be preserved.

The horror of the past few months came back to Freud

1

as he settled into the hard bunk of the Orient Express. The world had turned upside down since that day, three months earlier, when Nazi tanks had rumbled through the streets of Vienna. That was on March 15, 1938. Four days before, the Nazis had invaded Austria, taking one more giant step toward World War II. With their invasion had come the inevitable parade of storm troopers, marching through town after town, shouting their hated slogan, "Heil Hitler," before bewildered townspeople.

Soon after they arrived in Vienna the Nazis had made their way to Freud's quiet neighborhood. Working in his study, the old man had suddenly heard a commotion outside. Then there was the ugly sound of boots stomping past his doorway into his home. From his workroom he could hear his wife, in her sweet and gentle voice, inviting the intruders to be seated. He knew that her politeness must embarrass the brash young men who had come to loot his property, and he had smiled to himself.

The men had gone about their business, searching his safe and taking what valuables they could find. Suddenly, unable to control himself any longer, Freud had stalked into the room. As he stood there glaring, with burning eyes and scornful lips, even the Nazi conquerors had learned the meaning of fear. Without a word they had turned and left the house.

But Freud knew that his victory was short-lived. A week later the Nazis had returned, this time taking his youngest daughter Anna back with them to Gestapo headquarters. Even now the old man shuddered as he thought about that ordeal. All day he had paced up and down his room, smoking cigar after cigar, unable to speak to anyone. He had counted the minutes his Anna was away, and years had seemed to pass before she was returned, unharmed, at seven o'clock that night. Anna told of how she had been questioned over and over about her father's work, his writings, and his friends.

Now Freud had finally admitted to himself that he must take his family and leave his homeland forever. Until then he had hesitated, reluctant to abandon his country in its time of trouble. Every day he had looked for new excuses. He was too old and weak to travel. His reputation as a scientist would save him from harm. So many refugees were fleeing Europe that no country would have him.

Even while he argued, he knew there was no choice. Sigmund Freud was Jewish, and the Nazis had made the Jewish people their special targets. In the beginning they had been content to terrorize Jewish families, breaking into homes and looting stores. Then their madness had spread and their deeds had grown more gruesome. Every day that he stayed in Vienna, Freud saw the terror increase around him. Children were torn from their parents and shipped to labor yards to work as slaves. Adults were herded like animals into cattle cars without food or water, and sent miles away to concentration camps.

"I no longer understand this world," Freud had written to a friend.

It took a princess and a President to arrange Sigmund Freud's escape from Vienna. The Nazis were very strict about issuing passports. They did not want refugees streaming out of their conquered lands, telling the world of their inhuman deeds. For help, Freud had turned to Princess Marie Bonaparte of Greece, a descendant of the family of Napoleon I and a longtime friend of his. She paid the Nazis thousands of dollars in ransom money to gain permission for her friend to leave Austria and go to London. In the United States, which was still a neutral country, President Roosevelt heard of Sigmund Freud's plight. He instructed his ambassadors to do what they could to help the old man. To be doubly sure, Roosevelt used his personal influence to urge German diplomats to release Freud and his family. Freud had even heard that Benito Mussolini, dictator of Italy and ally of Adolf Hitler, had intervened to save him.

The train began to move, but the old man hardly noticed. He was deep in thought. How strange it was that a wealthy princess, the President of the most powerful country in the world, and the cruel dictator of an enemy nation had all worked to help him—an old, weak, dying man. Yet, for most of his life, he had not been able even to gain the respect of his own colleagues at the University of Vienna. For most of his life he had been mocked and cursed—or worse, simply ignored. Only now, in his later years, had his ideas been recognized and his name honored.

The world had been slow to accept Sigmund Freud. But then, Freud was not easy to accept. All his life he had been a rebel. At a time when people had little understanding of their feelings, he had delved deep into their minds and hearts and taught them to see themselves as they really were. At a time when dreams were laughed at or ignored, he had studied them carefully and shown them to have meaning that is as real and important as waking thoughts. At a time when men and women dared not speak of sex or family life, he had proved that their relationships to one another had a powerful influence on all their behavior.

Freud had opened up men's eyes and minds, and the world would never be the same because of him. He never accepted things on somebody else's word. He always had to explore for himself. His explorations had led to a whole new science—a science of the mind that he called psychoanalysis. A physician, Freud had used his techniques to cure the mentally ill. A teacher, he had gathered a group of followers and carefully taught them his methods and findings. A scientist, he had pressed on in his studies, even under the most painful conditions, always striving to unravel more and more of the mysteries of the human mind.

Freud's findings, which he published in dozens of books and journals, had shocked the people around him. For many years he had lived in isolation, not even allowed to lecture to his students. Then gradually the controversy and bitterness had died down. Slowly his fame had spread throughout the world until scientists and writers, housewives and politicians, had turned to him for advice and help.

Sigmund Freud had accepted the fame as he did the insults. He cared little about any of it. All that mattered was his work. That was why, an old and tired man, he had to leave his home. He had to stay alive as a symbol of the strength of his teachings. He had to live a little longer to finish the work he had begun so many years before. And he had to carry his studies to England, a land of freedom, where younger men could continue where he would leave off.

At three o'clock in the morning the train crossed the border from Germany into free France. A few days later, the trip ended in England, where the old refugee was led to safety. Sigmund Freud did not live very long in that strange new land, but the work to which he had devoted a lifetime has lived on to influence the thoughts and behavior of men, women, and children in all parts of the world.

CHAPTER TWO

A Wonderful Prophecy

From the beginning, Sigmund Freud's parents were sure that their son would grow up to be a great and famous man. Had the child not been born with a caul—an extra layer of skin around his skull? In those days people believed that this extra covering was a sure sign of future fame and happiness. Then, too, there was his head of thick black hair, so unusual for an infant. Together with his dark eyes it gave him a mysterious and Oriental look that led to his nickname of "little blackamoor."

Most important of all, there was the prophecy in the bakery shop.

Sigmund's mother often took her baby out with her when she went marketing. She loved to wheel his carriage from store to store, showing off her dark-eyed treasure to shopkeepers and neighbors. One day when Amalie Freud was in a bakery shop with her son an old peasant woman came in. The woman wore a long skirt, and a colorful babushka tied around her head. When she smiled, her face crinkled into hundreds of tiny lines and her mouth showed where several teeth were missing. The old woman leaned over little Sigi's carriage and began to play with the baby. As he cooed and gurgled, grabbing at her fingers and her hair, she kept looking at him closely. Then she turned to his mother and in a solemn, mysterious voice announced that the boy would one day be a great man.

To Amalie Freud this was exciting news, confirming her own belief that there was something special about her son. She rushed home to tell her husband about the incident. He teased her for being foolish enough to listen to a silly old woman, but secretly he felt proud that his son had been singled out. For many years afterward, the Freuds repeated the story of the old woman and her prophecy over and over. In fact, as he was growing up, young Sigmund heard it so often that even he came to think that perhaps, indeed, he was destined for something out of the ordinary in life.

It was not too unusual for the Freuds to believe in their old woman's vision of the future. They lived in a small town in Europe, far from the large cities and main cultural centers. Here, omens and signs, prophecies and predictions, were part of the everyday life of the people. Not that everybody believed wholeheartedly in fortune-telling—but most people did not find it difficult to accept a forecast of the future, especially when it was pleasant.

The town in which the Freuds lived was Freiberg, which was then part of the empire of Austria-Hungary and now is in Czechoslovakia. There Sigmund Freud was born on May 6, 1856, about five years before the Civil War began in the United States, during a period known as the Victorian Age in Europe.

Like Queen Victoria of England, for whom this period was named, the people of the time were prim and proper. Women wore long skirts down to their ankles, and high, starched collars. Men dressed in dark cutaway suits, often with tall silk hats. Large families were common, and children were taught to respect their elders —particularly their fathers, who demanded strict obedience. Some husbands and wives were so formal and stuffy that they addressed one another, even in private, as "Mr." and "Mrs." It is not surprising that the daring theories that Sigmund Freud developed many years later shocked the modest and self-righteous people of his time.

Sigmund's family did not differ much from other middle-class families. As in other families, there were a great many members. Sigmund's father, Jakob Freud, had married twice. His first wife had died, leaving him with two sons. His second wife—Amalie Nathansohn—bore him eight children: Sigmund was the oldest; then there were Julius, who died as an infant, five daughters—Anna, Rosa, Marie, Adolfine, and Paula—and another son, named Alexander.

A stately man, whom Sigmund grew up to resemble closely, Jakob Freud was a kind and affectionate father. He often took his son for walks in the beautiful meadow nearby, telling stories and anecdotes to the little boy who toddled along beside him. To Sigmund, his father was the "wisest and wealthiest" man who ever lived, but, in reality, Jakob was not wealthy at all. He earned his living as a wool merchant, and as his family grew he found it harder and harder to make ends meet. Warm and gentle by nature, Jakob rarely complained. He always expected that, somehow, the future would be better.

Perhaps it was his pleasant nature that led Jakob to choose as his second wife a woman twenty years younger than himself. Amalie Nathansohn, whom Jakob married when he was forty years old, was a gay, lively woman, born in a small town in Galicia, near Russia. Her happy laughter would ring through the Freud household, making little Sigi smile even in his saddest moods.

Throughout her life—and she lived to be ninety-five— no matter what misfortunes the family suffered, Amalie managed to keep her youthful good humor. Later, friends liked to remember that when she was ninety she refused to accept a shawl for her birthday because she was afraid it would make her look too old. And when she was ninety-five, shortly before she died, she complained bitterly about a picture of her that had been printed in a newspaper, because, she said, "It makes me look a hundred."

Only twenty-one when Sigmund was born, Amalie doted on her son. Although she loved all her children dearly, her "golden Sigi," as she called him, remained her favorite. And because she believed in the prophecy of the old woman, she treated him in a special way, as though he were a hero to be idolized. Protected and loved by his mother, young Sigmund grew up to feel confident of his own ability. Later, when he came to understand how important a mother's love is for a child, he wrote, "A man who has been the indisputable favorite of his mother keeps for life the feeling of a conqueror, that confidence of success that often induces real success." How different would his life have been, he often wondered, if his mother had treated him differently?

If Sigmund's mother spoiled him, his nursemaid made up for it in strictness. An ugly old woman, she had a rasping voice, which she used generously to scold the child when he got into mischief. Yet Sigi loved his old nurse. Sometimes, when she seemed to be in a good mood, he would crawl onto her lap and listen happily as she told him stories of her family and childhood. As a present, he would give her pennies he had carefully saved.

Deeply religious, the old nurse spent many hours teaching the child about good and evil. Over and over she described to him her visions of the joys of Heaven and the fiery punishment of Hell. On Sundays she would take Sigmund to church with her. Although the Freuds were Jewish, they did not observe many religious traditions, and they rarely attended synagogue services on Saturdays. For Sigmund, the Sunday outings to the tall church were a special treat. Once there, he would listen intently to the preacher's sermon, then come home and deliver a sermon of his own to his patient family.

One day Sigmund's nurse disappeared from the household, never to return. Much later, the heartbroken child was told that she had been caught stealing and had been sent to prison. The mystery of how the same person who had taught him so much about religion could herself commit an evil deed troubled the boy for a long time. Many years later, when Freud came to study his childhood as part of his psychoanalysis, he could still remember the influence of this "prehistoric old woman" and the shock of her sudden leave-taking.

There were other persons in Sigmund's childhood who influenced his later thought and development. There were his half brothers, Emmanuel and Philipp, each old enough to be his father, who helped care for him and teach him. There was also Emmanuel's son John, Sigmund's nephew, who was a year older than his uncle.

Sigmund and John became the best of friends, but for Sigmund the friendship was a difficult one. Smaller and frailer than John, he had to use all his energies to stand up to the older boy. And the strange fact that he was the uncle and John his nephew never ceased to puzzle him. Why did John call Sigmund's father "Grandpa"? Why was it that Sigmund's uncles were all much bigger and older than he, yet he was not big enough to lick his nephew? What made him hate John sometimes and love him at other times?

When the grown-up Freud looked back on this first friendship with John he realized how much it had influenced all the friendships that followed. Because of the combination of love and hate he had felt for John, he said, "An intimate friend and a hated enemy have always been indispensable to my emotional life." This childhood friendship with his nephew also helped Freud understand the confusing mixture of good and bad feelings that all friends and relatives have toward one another.

In spite of quarrels and childhood problems, life was pleasant for Sigmund, growing up in quiet little Freiberg. For Jakob Freud, though, the times became more and more difficult. The wool trade was declining steadily and the town itself was becoming poorer. New, larger industrial centers had grown up nearby, and railroads began to bypass the sleepy little town. Even more frightening for Jakob, a wave of anti-Semitism was spreading through the region—similar to the anti-Jewish feelings that swept Nazi Germany during Sigmund Freud's old age.

Fearing for his business and his family, Jakob decided to leave Freiberg for some place where his children could have a good education and a good life. In 1859, when Sigmund was three years old, the Freud family moved from Freiberg to Leipzig, a larger city in Germany. This move, Jakob believed, would make it possible for little Sigmund to achieve that greatness which the old woman in the bakery shop had predicted for him.

CHAPTER THREE

Growing Up in Vienna

The memory of the journey from Freiberg to Leipzig was to haunt Sigmund Freud for the rest of his life. The three-year-old boy understood little about the move. To him it was frightening and confusing. First he had to say good-bye to his nephew John, whose family also had decided to move, but to England rather than Germany. Then a horse-drawn carriage took Sigmund and his family far away from their comfortable house and the beautiful meadows where he had walked with his father.

It seemed like hours that they sat cramped in the carriage, headed for the railway station, to start the long journey toward an unknown new home. When they finally reached the station, the little boy's eyes opened wide with wonder. He had heard about trains and looked at pictures of them, but he had never actually seen one. Now the screaming locomotive whistle and the mountainous clouds of white smoke that rose from the engine fascinated and frightened him.

Once inside the train, he watched the landscape fly by as the family moved ever closer to a strange land. When the train passed through the little town of Breslau at night, Sigmund was terrified by the tall gas jets that lighted the station. All he could think of as he stared at the red and purple flames shooting up from the jets was his old nurse's horrible description of evil souls burning in a fiery Hell.

Like any child, Sigmund temporarily forgot about the long trip in the excitement of unpacking and settling into a new house. The mixed feelings of wonder and terror the journey had aroused remained buried deep inside him, however. For many years, as an adult, he had an uncontrollable phobia against trains—a fear of traveling on them. He finally traced his feelings back to that first fearful train ride when he had left his happy home in Freiberg.

The Freuds stayed in Leipzig just one year, then moved on to Vienna, Austria, where Jakob again hoped to better his position. At the time, Vienna was a bustling city and a cultural center of Europe. Here, as in other parts of Europe, Jews formed only a minority of the population, and were often severely persecuted because of their religion. But they had made some headway in achieving civil rights. By 1867, when Freud was eleven years old, they had been granted legal equality in the city. Many Jews had begun to enter professions that had once been closed to them, such as law and medicine, and in spite of continuing prejudice against them, some had become famous in their fields. Perhaps here, Jakob hoped, Sigmund's talents could flourish.

At first the family lived in a small apartment in the poor Jewish section of the city. Later, as more children arrived, they moved to larger quarters. Their new house was nice enough. It had a living room, dining room, and sufficient bedrooms for the family, but it lacked one essential—a bath! Once every two weeks, two hired hands would carry a huge wooden tub and several pitchers of hot water into the Freud kitchen, and there Sigmund and the other children would be bathed.

Sigmund had a special room of his own in the new home. Called the "cabinet," it was long and narrow, and separated from the rest of the house. Here the boy read, studied, and played. And here he lived during all his school years, treated with such respect by his family that only he had the privilege of using an oil lamp, while the others had to be satisfied with household candles.

Young Sigmund received his earliest education from his parents. First his mother, then his father handled his schooling. Although Jakob himself was largely self-taught, he was an intelligent and learned man, and he managed to instill in his son a great love for books and knowledge. Among other things, Jakob taught Sigmund to read the Bible regularly and to live by the moral lessons it contained.

At the age of nine, Sigmund passed a difficult examination and was accepted at the Sperl Gymnasium, an eight-year school comparable to a combination junior high and high school in the United States. The boy immediately excelled in his studies, and moved quickly to the head of his class. So brilliant was he, in fact, that his teachers exempted him from taking examinations or even being questioned often in class, making him the envy of his schoolmates.

Now reading and studying became the most important activities in Sigmund's life. He would rush home from school to his little "cabinet" and spend hours there, his elbows on his desk and a book propped up in front of him. Sometimes he became so absorbed in a subject that he would take his meals in his room to avoid breaking his train of thought.

As the young scholar progressed, the family's pride in him grew. Although sterner than his wife, even Jakob treated the boy leniently, allowing him to buy more books than the family could easily afford. Jakob could never hide his pride in his son's intelligence. Once when he was strolling through the street he saw a friend of Sigmund's arguing with his father. Jakob scolded the boy by saying, "What, are you contradicting your father? My Sigmund's little toe is cleverer than my head, but he would never dare to contradict me."

For Sigmund's comfort and education the Freuds were willing to make many sacrifices. In later life one of his sisters remembered an unhappy incident that took place during her childhood. Because Sigmund's mother loved music the family bought a piano, and the young girls began taking music lessons. But the sound of the music drifting into his room disturbed Sigmund in his studies. At his insistence the piano was removed from the house forever. After that, no member of the Freud family ever received a musical education. For the rest of his life, Freud disliked music, although he developed great love for art and other cultural forms.

In his own way, Sigmund tried to repay his family's indulgence of him. Just as his parents had taught him, he now taught his younger sisters. He carefully reviewed their lessons with them, and even instructed them in good manners and ladylike behavior. He took the role of "big brother" so seriously that he conscientiously censored the books his sisters read, to make sure they were quite proper for such young ladies.

Freud's sisters probably would have preferred their brother to be just a bit less brilliant and intellectual—especially as they grew older and became interested in the young men he brought home to visit. Sigmund would spirit his friends off to the "cabinet" for hours of serious discussion, never thinking that his pretty sisters might like to spend some time with them also.

There was much to attract Sigmund's friends to his room. His bookcases overflowed with writings on every subject imaginable. Special favorites on the shelves were military tales and histories of heroes of the past. Sigmund could spend hours reading about Hannibal and his daring march across the Alps or about Alexander the Great, whose armies conquered so many of the nations of the world during ancient times.

Sometimes Sigmund would dream of becoming a great general, and imagine himself leading battalions of men into bloody battle. When the Franco-Prussian War broke out in 1870 the boy bought a huge map on which he followed the battles with little flags. Then, in great detail, he would describe to his sisters just what was happening in each campaign.

Steeped in the heroic deeds of the past, Sigmund could never imagine himself being frightened or running away from difficulty. When he was twelve, his father told him a sad story of how a big, burly man had stalked over to him in the street and knocked his new hat into the mud. The man had cursed at him: "Jew, get off the pavement." Sigmund angrily demanded to know what his father had done in return. When Jakob quietly replied, "I stepped into the gutter and picked up my hat," the boy felt so ashamed and disappointed that he could barely look at his father. Although he continued to respect Jakob, he never regained his earlier admiration for the older man, and he vowed that in his own life he would always fight back, no matter who his attacker might be.

But battles and war heroes were only one part of young Freud's interests. Indeed, as time went on, they faded into the background against his burning love of all learning. With a natural gift for languages, Sigmund mastered not only his native German, but also Latin and Greek. He taught himself Italian and Spanish, and acquired a special love for English. At the age of eight, when most children are just beginning to read simple stories for themselves, Freud "discovered" the writings of William Shakespeare. He soon read everything the playwright had written, and throughout his life delighted in quoting in English from Shakespeare.

Another favorite author was Mark Twain. Freud first became familiar with American literature and with the United States at the International Exhibition in Vienna, a world's fair that took place in 1873. Sigmund was only seventeen at the time, but he was so impressed with the

American Constitution and the *Gettysburg Address*, which he saw at the American pavilion, that he bought copies of them and read them out loud to his sisters. Later, he hung a copy of the *Declaration of Independence* above his bed.

In spite of his dedication to his studies, young Sigmund managed to find time to relax and have fun, too. He liked to swim, and in the winter enjoyed ice skating with his friends. But mostly he loved to walk. He and his father took long walks through the streets and surrounding neighborhoods of Vienna, much as they used to walk when he was a little boy in Freiberg. Often Sigmund went hiking alone in the nearby mountains, thinking seriously about himself and his future as he marched briskly along.

The future became more and more important as little Sigi grew into a mature young man. Graduation from the Gymnasium was approaching. Sigmund knew that he had to decide on a course in life and begin preparing for it. It would be a difficult decision to make, and one that the elder Freuds left entirely to their son.

CHAPTER FOUR

Medical Student

How do you go about choosing a career when you are seventeen, the oldest in a family of limited means, and expected to achieve great things? Young Freud did not know. There *had* been those early dreams of becoming a famous military leader, but they had faded as he became more absorbed in his studies. Then there lurked in his mind a vague idea of becoming a lawyer or a government official—an idea that stemmed, strangely enough, from a second prophecy about his future.

That prophecy had occurred when Sigmund was about eleven or twelve years old. He and his family were enjoying a festive dinner at a town restaurant. As they ate they noticed a man moving from table to table and amusing the people for a small fee by making up verses on any subject given him. Sigmund was sent to fetch the "poet" to the Freud table. Before asking for a subject, the man took a long, hard look at the young boy. Then without hesitating, he composed some rhymes about Sigmund, hinting that the youth would grow up to be an important minister in the government.

Like the prophecy of the old woman in the bakery

shop, this second prediction about Sigmund's future delighted the Freuds. They knew that only in recent years had members of middle-class families like their own been appointed to positions in the government. Until then, that honor had been reserved for the aristocracy or the very rich. How nice it would be for their Sigmund to become a government minister!

But somehow Sigmund knew that law and government did not really suit him. During his last years in high school he felt a "sort of curiosity" growing within him, a desire to know as much as possible about the universe and about the men who inhabit it. Now science began to intrigue him. He became particularly interested in the writings of Charles Darwin, whose theory of evolution had recently aroused a storm of controversy in scientific circles. To Freud, Darwin's theories "held out hopes of an extraordinary advance in our understanding of the world."

With this interest in science deepening, it took just a minor incident to set Sigmund Freud on his lifelong course of medical and scientific study. Toward the end of his final school semester he heard an essay on nature by the German poet Wolfgang von Goethe read aloud at a lecture. The essay described nature in beautiful, romantic terms as a mother who allows only her favorite children to explore her mysteries. So moved was Freud by this description and so anxious to become one of the "children" privileged to explore nature that, he later wrote, hearing the essay "decided me to become a medical student."

Freud graduated from the Gymnasium in 1873, with the highest honor, *summa cum laude*. As a reward for his outstanding scholastic achievement his father promised him a trip to England—a trip that he made and enjoyed immensely two years later. Shortly after graduation, the seventeen-year-old boy entered the University of Vienna as a medical student.

Right from the start, Freud saw his medical studies simply as a means of gaining an understanding of science and of learning the disciplines and techniques of scientific investigation. Medicine as an end in itself held little interest for him, and the idea of becoming a practicing physician interested him even less.

He took his required medical courses with little enthusiasm, and later admitted that during those first years at the university, "I was compelled to make the discovery that the peculiarities and limitations of my gifts denied me all success in many of the departments of science into which my youthful eagerness had plunged me."

Then, suddenly, in his fourth year the young medical student's interest perked up—so much so, that he later extended his medical studies three extra years. The reason for this new interest was a brilliant, iron-willed professor of physiology named Ernst Brücke. The professor became an idol of Freud's. Brücke was "the greatest authority," exclaimed Freud, and in his physiology laboratory the youth found "rest and satisfaction."

That anyone could find "rest" in the presence of Ernst Brücke would have surprised many of Freud's schoolmates. A short man with a large head and thin lips,

Brücke had steel-blue eyes that could strike terror into the hearts of even his boldest students. Once, when Freud came to class late, Brücke scolded him and then fixed him with an icy stare that left the young man "overwhelmed." In later years just the memory of those piercing blue eyes was enough to prevent Freud from being lazy in carrying out some piece of research.

Brücke had the reputation of being the most difficult of all professors, especially during oral examinations. If a pupil missed the first question, the professor would refuse to go on. He would simply sit out the rest of the examination period in cold, angry silence, shutting his ears to the pleadings of the unfortunate student.

But there was another side to Ernst Brücke that Freud came to know and love. A man of great honesty, Brücke was completely dedicated to seeking scientific truth. He had little ambition to achieve fame and honor for himself. As a result, he was willing to encourage his students to experiment on their own, even if their results might prove him wrong. Brücke had great respect for those students who, like Freud, worked hard and were earnest in their studies. Like a father, he advised them and helped them in their work and in their personal lives.

Freud's courses with Brücke were held in the professor's Institute of Physiology, a group of classrooms and laboratories housed in an old gun factory. Dark and gloomy, the Institute had miserable accommodations. Its almost windowless rooms lacked heat, and the only water available came from a well in the yard. Yet the young scientist could hardly wait to return to the building each day. He bitterly regretted the hours he had to spend in the far more comfortable university classrooms—studying such subjects as surgery and pathology.

As a research project, Brücke set Freud to work examining the nerve cells of simple animals. Although the student's task was a limited one, it was part of an important and far-reaching argument going on in the field of physiology.

Scientists wanted to know how the nervous system—and with it the mind—of man and the higher animals differed from that of the lower animals. Were both systems made up of the same basic substances, differing mainly in the number of nerve cells and their arrangement? Or were the minds of higher animals composed of completely different elements from those of lower animals?

Through exacting microscopic studies of the crayfish and other simple animals, Freud discovered that there was, indeed, a very close relationship between the cells in the nervous systems of lower animals and those of higher animals. The findings and techniques that Freud published proved an important contribution to the field of neurology, which deals with the makeup and function of nerve cells.

Young Freud's first scientific ventures show little of the boldness and imagination that became typical of his later work, however. For the present he was content to describe things as he saw them and to stay within accepted traditions in presenting his conclusions. How greatly he would change in later years when, without hesitation, he toppled all traditions and developed his own psychoanalytical theory of the mind!

Freud's scientific studies were interrupted in 1879 when he was called up to serve a year of compulsory military duty in the Austro-Hungarian army. To pass the time when he was not busy in the army hospital, he translated into German a book of essays by the British writer John Stuart Mill.

His old flair for languages came back to him in preparing the translation. He would read a section, then shut the book and figure out in his mind how a German writer might have expressed the same thought. The result was a beautiful and lively work, unlike the stilted phrase-by-phrase translations common for the time.

When Freud returned to the university and Brücke's laboratory in 1880 he planned to pick up where he had left off in his scientific research. He also decided finally to take the examinations necessary for obtaining a medical degree, even if he would never put that degree to practical use. With little studying he managed to pass almost all his examinations with the grade of "excellent." He later confessed that he was one of those few persons lucky enough to have a photographic memory. While others struggled through their textbooks, Freud could remember things he had read or even glanced at once.

With the examinations out of the way, twenty-five-year-old Sigmund Freud received his medical degree on March 30, 1881.

At first, nothing changed. Freud won an appointment as a junior member of the staff of his beloved Institute of Physiology and set out to continue his scientific research. Thin, yet sturdy, with intense dark eyes and a thick black beard, he looked every bit the serious and dedicated young scientist. But his dreams of a scientific career were soon shattered by the practical, everyday necessity of earning a living. And it was Professor Brücke, of all people, who brought him face to face with reality.

How, Brücke wanted to know, did Freud plan to support himself during the coming years? The Institute paid almost nothing, and Freud had no outside source of income. His father, who had financed his studies for years, had lost almost all his money in an economic crash during the 1870's. Old and unable to earn much himself, Jakob had to borrow from his wife's family to support his many dependents. There was little he could do to help his son now. Rather, Freud would soon have to take on some of the responsibilities of caring for the family.

Would it not be better, Brücke pointed out, for Freud to give up his plans for a career in science and open a medical practice where he could earn a good living?

Reluctantly, Freud had to agree with his adviser. In July, 1882, he resigned from the Institute of Physiology to begin preparing for a medical career. But not even Professor Brücke knew the very special reason that had finally pushed him to make the painful "separation from science." That reason was a gay young girl from Hamburg with whom the studious scientist had fallen head over heels in love. To marry her he must have some means of support.

CHAPTER FIVE

"Princess" Martha

Martha Bernays managed to capture Freud's heart at their very first meeting. She and her sister were visiting with Freud's sisters one evening when the young doctor returned from the laboratory. Usually Freud retired to his room immediately, but the sight of the pretty, dark-haired girl drew him to the living room, much to the surprise of his family. He watched her as she talked and laughed, her eyes sparkling and her voice vivacious, and he knew at once that this was the girl he would someday marry.

Twenty-one years old when they met that evening in April, 1882, Martha was five years younger than Freud. Pale and petite, she had a delicate beauty that reminded Freud of a fragile china doll, yet she was strong-willed and intelligent, with a quick wit and gracious manner that won her many beaux.

Martha came from a highly educated and well-known family in Hamburg, Germany. Her grandfather had been the chief rabbi of Hamburg during the early 1800's, and her father, a merchant, had reared his children in strict religious practices. The family moved from Hamburg to

Vienna in 1869, when Martha was eight years old. Ten years later her father died and her brother Eli took over his business position. But Martha's mother, a strong, dominating woman, became the real head of the family, demanding unquestioning obedience from her children.

Freud knew that as a suitor he would be unacceptable to Martha's mother, both because he was poor and because he held liberal religious views that differed greatly from the traditional practices of the Bernays family. He was determined to win the girl's love, however, and he lost no time in courting her.

He began by sending her a red rose every day, with a little poem or proverb attached. Then the couple arranged to meet for long walks in the country, on which they were often accompanied by Martha's mother or brother. Soon the meetings grew more private, and the gifts Freud sent his love became more meaningful.

Early in June, Freud wrote Martha his first letter, beginning with the words "My sweet darling girl." In it he confessed his deep feelings for her and his hope that she shared those feelings. Apparently she did. In response to his letter she presented him with a ring that had belonged to her father, and he had a duplicate made for her. On Saturday, June 17, just two months after their first meeting, the couple agreed to consider themselves engaged.

Now began a long period of hardship and separation that lasted almost five years before the two were married. During that time, Freud wrote more than nine hundred letters to his "Princess," his pet name for Martha. The letters tell of his strong passion, his unreasoning jealousy, and the poverty and unhappiness he suffered. Martha considered those letters so personal and precious that many years later, after Freud's death, she planned to burn them. Only her daughter's pleading saved them to become a treasured record of Sigmund Freud's early life and thoughts.

At first the young couple planned to keep their engagement a secret from Martha's family, who would surely object to it. They met only from time to time, and stealthily exchanged letters. Impatient in his passion, Freud bitterly resented the circumstances that prevented him from seeing his love more often. He even threatened to have an out-and-out confrontation with Martha's mother, who, he said, "is fascinating; but alien, and will always remain so to me." He grew furious at even the slightest hint of a friendship between Martha and other men, and bombarded her with questions—mentally torturing himself until the answers arrived.

"Just think," he wrote, "half the time that passes between my question and your answer . . . [is] so drawn out by harrowing thoughts about you that in the end a poor man can't distinguish an hour from a month or a year."

The situation was to become much worse before it became better. The couple's families finally guessed their secret, and Martha's mother reluctantly announced her acceptance of her future son-in-law. But now, secretly hoping that distance would cool the romance, she decided to move her family back to Hamburg. No amount of pleading or angry demands on the part of Freud or Martha would change her mind.

In June, 1883, a year after their engagement, Freud said a sad farewell to Martha and promised to visit her whenever he could, and to write faithfully every day.

Impatiently Freud looked forward to the day when he and Martha would wed, but they both knew that the wait would be a long one. Almost all of Freud's training had been in scientific research and laboratory work, with little experience in actually treating patients. In order to open a medical practice with private patients he would have to get that experience by working in a hospital clinic for at least two years. Even when that training period ended, it would be some time before he earned enough money in his practice to be able to afford marriage.

Because it was unheard of for a young woman of a good family to go to work, the entire burden of earning and saving money fell on Freud. He would have to struggle and suffer, putting away whatever little he could toward their future.

And suffer he did! He made Martha his banker and regularly sent her small sums of money that he managed somehow to put aside from the miserable hospital allowance he received. Each day he wrote her an accounting of just how he had spent his money, discussing with her such small matters as buying a necktie or a handkerchief. Sometimes Freud would have to wear his clothes until they had holes in them, in the meanwhile borrowing a suit or jacket from a more well-to-do friend in order to go out.

Added to Freud's anxiety about money was the terrible poverty of his family. His father, now close to seventy, had stopped earning any income. His sisters grew thin and emaciated, and his mother began to suffer from tuberculosis. Freud gave his parents as much as he could, and once in a while they were able to borrow from relatives. Somehow they managed to survive, but their desperate situation constantly worried their son.

As the days went on and the weeks of separation grew into months and years, Freud's loneliness and longing became more intense. In his letters he poured out his love for Martha.

"In the early days my love for you was mingled with bitter pain," he told her, "then later came the cheerful confidence of lasting loyalty and friendship, and now I love you with a kind of passionate enchantment which is the only feeling left and which has exceeded my expectations."

He grew angry at any imagined sign of coldness on her part, then apologized by saying, "One is very crazy when one is in love." Sometimes, to draw their wedding day closer, he would describe to her in great detail how their future would be: ". . . we would need two little rooms where we can live and eat and receive a guest, and a stove in which the fire for our meals never goes out. . . . There will be so much to enjoy, the books, the sewing table and the cozy lamp."

On rare occasions when Freud could borrow or earn some extra money through tutoring, he would visit Martha. Those few times when he was able to scrape together

enough to buy her a small present—usually a book—he
considered the "greatest moments." He loved to write
and talk to her about books and about his own philosophy of life. Shyly and proudly he told her once of a re-
mark made about him by a well-known physician in
Vienna: "He told me he had discovered that hidden
under the surface of timidity there lay in me an extremely
fearless and daring human being. I had always thought
so, but never dared tell anyone."

The "fearless and daring" traits that lay buried inside
Freud did not extend, however, to matters that concerned Martha. He worried that she might become impressed by the movements for women's rights that had
sprung up throughout Europe, and made clear to her
that he shared the strict Victorian attitudes of most men
of his time.

To "protect" her, he censored the books Martha read,
as he had censored his sisters' books. He even forbade her
to go skating in a group if it meant that she would have to
hold another man's arm. Typical of the modesty and
prudishness of the day, he was very cautious in compli-
menting her beauty. Once he apologized in a letter for
noticing her tiny feet, because proper gentlemen did not
look at or mention that part of the body.

The long years of separation and letter writing finally
ended in 1886, when Sigmund Freud was thirty and his
beloved Martha was twenty-five. On September 13, the
couple was married in a civil ceremony in Wandsbek,
near Hamburg. The next day a religious ceremony took
place. Freud had built up a modest practice, and the

newlyweds began their life together in a four-room flat in Vienna.

They lived together for more than fifty years, sharing an unusually happy marriage. After their first child was born in 1887, Freud wrote a friend, "We live pretty happily in steadily increasing unassumingness. When we hear the baby laugh we imagine it is the loveliest thing that can happen to us."

In all, the Freuds had six children: Mathilde, born in 1887; Jean Martin, in 1889; Oliver, in 1891; Ernst, in 1892; Sophie, in 1893; and Anna, in 1895.

An addition to the household from 1896 on was Martha's spinster sister Minna. Adored by the Freud children, "Tante Minna" was a brilliant and witty woman. Freud enjoyed discussing his ideas and work with her, while he depended on his more domestic wife to run their home and care for him and the children.

Throughout the ups and downs of Freud's long life he remained a gentle and loving father and a kind and considerate husband. Above everything else, his family, he always said, was his "pride" and his "riches."

The Cocaine Experiments

When Sigmund Freud gave up his scientific career in 1882, determined to begin a private medical practice, he had no definite ideas about what fields of medicine most interested him. The only thing he was sure about was his desire to earn enough money to marry and support his Martha.

To get the practical training he needed, Freud enrolled in July, 1882, in the General Hospital of Vienna. For the next three years he rotated from one hospital service to another, gathering first-hand experience in many fields of medicine.

Of them all, one service made the strongest—and worst —impression on Freud. That was the department of nervous diseases, headed by a Doctor Franz Scholz. Here were grouped patients with a wide range of illnesses. Some had actual physical diseases that affected various parts of their bodies and nervous systems, but a great many had nothing wrong with their bodies. Today physicians would say that their illnesses were caused by emotional and mental problems rather than physical ailments, but until Freud's own discoveries, doctors knew very little about mental illnesses. They blamed these illnesses on damage in the brain or some part of the nervous system. Even when they could find no physical cause for a disturbance, they simply labeled it a "nervous disease," and treated the patient as they happened to think fit.

As chief, Doctor Scholz aimed to run his service "efficiently" by keeping costs down as much as possible. He allowed his staff to prescribe only the cheapest medicines, and often let his patients go hungry. The wards were filthy and unlighted. In the evenings the patients lay in complete darkness, and the physicians had to use lanterns while making their rounds or even performing emergency operations.

Freud was sickened by the conditions he saw, and bothered by the lack of care given to the "nervous" patients. For the moment, as he moved from one service to the next, he could do little to change the situation, but the short time he spent in those dismal wards left a lasting impression on him.

In addition to his work on the hospital wards, Freud found time to continue some of his research and scientific studies, particularly on the nervous system and the brain. Secretly he dreamed of making a brilliant discovery that would lead to quick fame and wealth and hasten his wedding day.

By 1884, Freud had reason to believe he was approaching his goal. He had heard of a new drug called cocaine that was made from the leaves of the coca tree. South American Indians were said to chew coca leaves to give themselves energy and lift their spirits. Would it be

possible, Freud wondered, for the drug to have the same effect, curing the sick and strengthening the weak?

Today physicians know that cocaine is a valuable but also a dangerous drug. Its most common use is in the compound, novocaine, an anesthetic that dentists and surgeons use to numb parts of the body during painful procedures. Taken in large doses, cocaine can become habit-forming and eventually cause illness and even death.

In Freud's day, nobody had yet investigated the drug cocaine. Actually, the whole field of drugs had barely been opened. There were few scientific procedures established for studying the effects of drugs, and almost no laws regulating their use and sale. To carry out their experiments, most scientists used themselves as guinea pigs —some sacrificing their lives for the noble cause of science.

In the finest tradition of his time, Freud set out to discover the properties of cocaine by swallowing small doses of the drug himself. To his surprise he found that it made him feel lighthearted. It caused his headaches and bad moods to disappear, and helped him concentrate on his work for longer periods of time than ever before. So pleased was he with its results that he sent small amounts to Martha, and convinced—almost forced—his friends and family to take cocaine whenever they could afford to buy some.

Every day, Freud found more and more uses for cocaine. It helped digestion. It numbed pain. It cured nausea. And best of all, it seemed perfectly harmless. He experienced no unpleasant side effects and felt no craving for it, as persons do when they become addicted to a drug. Surely this must be a "magical drug," Freud reasoned, never realizing that the amounts he had taken were too small to cause serious harm.

Now it occurred to Freud that cocaine could serve as a substitute for the drug morphine, which until then had been the chief pain-killer used by physicians. An extremely powerful drug, morphine easily causes addiction so that persons who take it over a long period of time have an uncontrollable desire for it.

To learn more about his "wonderful" drug and at the same time perform a humanitarian deed, Freud began giving cocaine to a dear friend, Ernst Fleischl. Handsome and brilliant, Fleischl was a tragic hero of medicine. While conducting research in a laboratory, he had contracted an incurable infection. To save his life, his thumb and then more and more of his hand had to be amputated. Still the infection continued to spead throughout his body so that he lived in constant, agonizing pain.

Fleischl had become addicted to morphine, which he took regularly in huge doses to kill his unbearable pain. His addiction led to sleepless nights, fainting spells, and attacks of trembling. Gradually Freud began to substitute cocaine for the morphine, and Fleischl's symptoms seemed to disappear. He used less and less morphine, and for many weeks appeared healthier than he had been in a long time.

Delighted with his results, in 1884 Freud published

a short paper on cocaine, in which he described in glowing terms the qualities he had observed. The work was an immediate success. From all parts of the world, physicians began writing to him for more information on his remarkable discovery. He was invited to lecture on cocaine before scholarly audiences, and to carry out experiments for drug companies in Europe and the United States. For a while, Freud's dreams of fame and wealth seemed to come true.

Then something happened. Quietly, at first, criticism of the drug started to appear in medical journals. One physician reported a case of cocaine addiction. Another described a fit of trembling which a cocaine user had experienced. Still another blamed his patient's death on an overdose of cocaine. The reports of cocaine poisoning and addiction increased until a storm of criticism against Freud and his drug broke out in medical journals. He had misunderstood the strength of the "miracle" drug. He had carelessly misrepresented his drug as being harmless. He had, in fact, according to one authority, unleashed a new "scourge" upon mankind.

At first, Freud tried to defend his paper and his results with cocaine. Soon he had to admit that his critics were quite right. Taken over long periods of time in large amounts, cocaine could be a terrible and dangerous drug. One of Freud's own patients had died suddenly from its use, and after his promising beginning, Fleischl had become so incurably addicted to it that he was spending thousands of Austrian marks to buy the drug. Fleischl's old symptoms had returned, and such painful new ones had appeared that Freud had to spend long nights caring for his tormented friend.

Shamed by his mistake, and with his dreams of glory shattered, Freud later suppressed his cocaine paper, refusing to mention it in writing or speaking. Although today scientists hail his early experiments as an important breakthrough in understanding the use of cocaine, the sensitive physician never forgave himself for his mistake.

As fate would have it, in the one area where cocaine became immediately useful, Freud received little credit for his work. He had thought the drug might be used successfully as an anesthetic in eye operations and had hoped to carry out some experiments along those lines. At the time, however, he was anxious to leave on a long-awaited vacation and visit with Martha.

Instead of doing the experiments himself, Freud mentioned his idea to some friends who specialized in the study of the eye. One of them, Carl Koller, made careful studies of the drug's effect on the eyes, proving that Freud's theory was a sound one. For his work, Koller won lasting recognition as the first person to find a simple and safe way to anesthetize the eye.

Although Freud congratulated his friend heartily on his achievement, he bitterly regretted his own "laziness." Forty years later, in describing the incident in his autobiography, he wrote, half seriously, that "it was the fault of my fiancée that I was not already famous at that early age." But, he added later, "I bore my fiancée no grudge for her interruption of my work."

In spite of the cocaine blunders, Freud's professional

standing gradually advanced as a result of his research and clinical work. Early in 1885 he was appointed a Docent at the University of Vienna—a highly respected title that earned him the right to lecture to university students. Meanwhile his interest in nervous diseases kept growing. To satisfy that interest he applied for a grant to study in Paris under a famous physician named Jean Martin Charcot. With the help of his beloved Professor Brücke he received the grant.

In October, 1885, Freud set out excitedly for Paris, promising Martha that as a result of this trip ". . . we will soon get married and I will cure all the incurable nervous cases." He could not guess that those next few months in Paris would prove to be a turning point in his life, setting him on the path of his greatest achievement.

CHAPTER SEVEN

Hypnotism and Hysteria

Paris, the cultural capital of the world, the city of fashion and fine food, of love and scandal, of art, literature, and drama. Paris. To twenty-nine-year-old Sigmund Freud it was an overwhelming city, a "magically attractive and repulsive city." Even the people here were different. Outspoken, emotional, often lighthearted, they bore little resemblance to the somber, hardworking Germans whom Freud had known all his life. Next to the Parisians, he felt like a country bumpkin on his first visit to a big city. Every day he found new and fascinating sights and events to describe in long letters to Martha.

Most fascinating were the hours he spent at the famous Salpêtrière, the clinic in which Jean Charcot treated nervous diseases and lectured to students from all parts of the world. The building itself had an important history. More than a hundred years before Freud's time it had served as an insane asylum—a cruel, forbidding institution where the mentally ill were herded together like animals. Because people did not understand mental sickness, they had believed the insane to be possessed of devils and evil spirits.

At the Salpêtrière and other mental institutions, patients had been chained to the walls, beaten, starved, and tortured to "free" them of their "demons." Then, in the 1790's, a French physician named Philippe Pinel had begun a long uphill struggle for more humane treatment of the mentally sick. In the Salpêtrière, in the very halls where Freud attended lectures and studied cases, Pinel had impressed the world by dramatically striking the chains from the tormented patients.

Looking around him, Freud could see how much progress had been made in the care and treatment of mental illness since Pinel's day, but he knew that many problems remained unanswered. He remembered the poor care given to patients at the General Hospital in Vienna, and he still puzzled over the wide range of illnesses he and other physicians nonchalantly classified as nervous diseases. Now, in these tradition-steeped wards, he hoped to gain new understanding and to learn new medical techniques that he could demonstrate to his colleagues at home.

He was not disappointed. Jean Charcot had made a worldwide reputation as a neurologist, an expert in the study of nerves. Brilliant and witty, he kept his students enthralled as he lectured to them on every manner of nervous disease, classifying and describing symptoms unexplained by other neurologists. Freud found Charcot's talks so impressive that within a few days he was able to write home that "no other human being has ever affected me in the same way."

At the time of Freud's visit, Charcot was devoting

most of his attention to the study of a strange, yet common, illness that had baffled physicians for years. The illness was called hysteria, and it took many forms. A patient suffering from hysteria complained of all sorts of physical ailments. Often an arm or leg was paralyzed. Sometimes the patient could not move his head, or swallow. In other cases, various parts of the body felt numb. Some hysterical patients even suffered severe convulsions. Yet, no matter how thoroughly these patients were examined, no one could find a physical cause for their symptoms. The patients' bones, muscles, nerves, and organs were healthy, but they functioned as though they had been injured.

This was certainly a puzzling condition—so much so, that most doctors chose to ignore it entirely. "The patient is pretending to be ill in order to gain attention," was a common explanation. Another explanation was that the patient just "imagined" that he felt numb or could not move. Because a large number of hysterical patients were women, many doctors simply shrugged the whole illness off as "some female trouble" and let it go at that.

For the great Charcot, none of these explanations sufficed. Too many patients suffered from the symptoms of hysteria to dismiss them as pretended or imaginary ailments. And enough men were stricken with hysterical illnesses for Charcot to know that this was not strictly a woman's complaint. But if there was nothing wrong with a patient's body, what caused him to take on symptoms of physical illness? Even Charcot could not answer that. What he could do, however, was treat a patient's symptoms even if he did not know what caused them, and he could do it in a completely different way from that used by anyone before him. Unlike other neurologists, Charcot did not search for medicines or body remedies to cure hysteria. Because the symptoms seemed to spring from the patient's mind rather than his body, Charcot looked for ways to influence that mind. The method he found most effective was as radical as his entire approach to hysteria. That method was hypnotism.

There was nothing new about the concept of hypnotism when Charcot began using it in the 1880's. As early as the 1700's it had been described by an Austrian physician named Franz Mesmer as a way to treat illness. It had even been known at first as mesmerism. But the practice had quickly become associated with quackery because it was used so much by unethical persons who claimed to be able to perform "miraculous" cures with it.

Hypnotism had aroused new interest in the 1840's when an English medical writer, James Braid, made a scientific investigation of it. Braid was the first person to use the term, "hypnotism," and to describe the deep trance a hypnotized person experiences. In spite of Braid's work, most medical men continued to have a low opinion of hypnotism as a technique in treating illness. Many thought it too "unscientific" to be worth while. Others considered it useless, even dangerous.

Then along came Jean Charcot, and—agree or not—no one could deny his results. Together with dozens of other observers, Freud watched in admiration as Charcot put his hysterical patients into a deep, hypnotic trance. Then, gradually, the famous physician would attack one symptom after another. Speaking softly, he would assure the patient over and over that the symptom had disappeared. And amazingly, so it had. A patient who had felt paralyzed in the legs when awake could walk normally when under hypnosis he was told to do so by Charcot. A patient who could not raise his arms would be able to carry heavy weights during the hypnotic state.

Perhaps even more impressive, Charcot was able to produce hysterical symptoms in patients who had none before. He could make a patient experience paralysis or convulsions exactly like those of hysteria. Then, with a few words, he could make the symptoms disappear again.

To Sigmund Freud, Charcot's dramatic demonstrations and his pronouncements on hysteria opened up a whole new world. Although in later years he broke away from Charcot's hypnotic technique, he always regarded Charcot with the greatest respect and admiration. One of Freud's most treasured possessions throughout his life was a print he brought away with him from the Salpêtrière. It showed Charcot hypnotizing a hysterical patient before an awed group of visiting physicians.

In February, 1886, Freud left Paris after a stay of only four and a half months instead of the six months he had been allowed on his grant. In spite of his fascination with Charcot and the excitement of the city itself, the young lover's longing for his Martha had become unbearable. Then, too, he was impatient to share his new knowledge with his teachers and colleagues in Vienna. He also wanted to try out for himself the daring techniques he had learned at the Salpêtrière.

Filled with enthusiasm on his return to Vienna, Freud immediately began preparing a paper to present before the city's medical society. Called "On Male Hysteria," the paper described in great detail the cases of hysteria in men that Freud had witnessed in Paris. Excitedly the young man waited for an opportunity to read his paper. He fully expected that he would be applauded and honored for the new evidence he had to show on hysteria in men, not just women.

That opportunity came on October 15, 1886, about a month after Freud's wedding to Martha. Before a distinguished audience that included many of his former professors at the University of Vienna, Freud nervously began reading his paper. Immediately he sensed something wrong. Nobody smiled as he spoke. Nobody nodded approval as he presented his exciting information. The faces before him stared back coldly, and icy silence greeted his words.

They didn't believe him! Even those few who did, cared little. Charcot was a Frenchman. How dare Freud —just a young upstart—try to teach his own professors something he had learned in a foreign land, and a land that had been a traditional enemy of Austria, at that!

During the question period after his lecture, Freud was attacked from all sides. How did he know the cases he had seen were really cases of hysteria? Wasn't it possible that his so-called hysterical men really suffered from brain

damage? Didn't he know that hysteria had *always* been
connected with women—as far back as ancient times?

Most outspoken in his criticism of Freud's paper was
Theodor Meynert, a specialist in brain anatomy, and
head of the Psychiatric Clinic at the General Hospital.
Freud had spent two years working under Meynert during his training period at the hospital, and a feeling of
mutual respect had grown up between the two men. But
now Meynert challenged Freud to find a case of male
hysteria in Vienna similar to those he had described.
After a futile search, Meynert assured the others, Freud
would drop all his "nonsense" about male hysteria.

Meynert had not reckoned on Freud's determination,
however. In just a few weeks, Freud returned before the
society and presented his case. "This time," he wrote
years later in his autobiography, "I was applauded, but no
further interest was taken in me. The impression that the
high authorities had rejected my innovations remained
unshaken; and . . . I found myself forced into the Opposition." It was his first taste of the strong, unrelenting
opposition that would greet all his new ideas concerning
mental illness.

Now Meynert became Freud's chief enemy. Jealous of
Freud's unswerving loyalty to the Frenchman Charcot,
he did not miss an occasion to attack the younger man.
He even excluded Freud from his cerebral anatomy laboratory, where the young Docent had lectured to medical
students.

Meynert was particularly angered at Freud's growing
interest in hypnotism which, he said, "degrades" a man.

And as far as hysteria was concerned, Meynert looked for ways to discredit Freud's findings whenever possible. Male hysteria just did not exist, he insisted. The illness in men that Freud had labeled hysteria was strictly a physical one that stemmed from some brain damage.

Meynert's anger and brutal attacks surprised and hurt Freud, who had always admired the professor. The young man could not know then the deep, frightening secret that lay behind Meynert's bitterness. Freud learned that secret a few years later. In 1892, when Meynert lay on his deathbed, he sent for his former student. There, in the strictest confidence, he told Freud that he himself had been a typical case of male hysteria. He had hidden his symptoms from everyone, and feared that Freud's research and open discussion of male hysteria might expose him. Now, close to death, he wanted Freud to know the truth.

In spite of criticism and attacks, Freud's interest in hypnotism continued to grow. He wrote papers on hypnotism, reviewed books about it, and used it frequently in treating the nervous patients who came to see him in his office.

Then, during the summer of 1889, he made a trip to Nancy, a small city in France, to observe the work of two physicians, Ambroise-August Liébault and Hippolyte Bernheim. These two dedicated men had worked among the poor people of that town for many years and had used hypnotism as an important tool in curing illnesses. In their hospital, Freud studied notes on more than ten thousand patients who had been hypnotized. He also watched hypnotic experiments, not only with hysteria, but with many kinds of mental conditions. More than ever, he came to feel that a great number of the nervous diseases he and his colleagues in Vienna had been treating had little to do with actual diseases of the nerves. The mind, rather than the body, was the key to these illnesses.

Back home again, Freud began to build up a prosperous medical practice. He had opened the practice in April, 1886, five months before his marriage. By training, Freud was prepared to treat many kinds of illnesses, and he saw patients with a wide variety of physical complaints. But by and large, the greatest number of his patients were nervous patients who, he said, "hurried, with their troubles unsolved, from one physician to another."

Still, Freud was not yet ready to confine his work to these nervous patients who had no physical illness. In addition to his medical practice, he became director of the neurological department of the Kassowitz Institute for Children's Diseases and spent several hours a day working there and earning a reputation as an expert in children's illnesses. He continued his laboratory research on brain anatomy and nerve tissues, and he somehow found time to write a book on speech defects—a side interest he had acquired. Called *Aphasia*, the book was published in 1891. It sold very few copies at the time and earned only sixty dollars in royalties for Freud. Today, experts consider it a pioneer work in the understanding of speech defects in children and adults.

That book, Freud's first, was also the last he wrote in the field of neurology. By the 1890's, he finally decided to give up his research and experiments in the physical aspects of medicine and to concentrate all his attention on discovering the causes and treatment of nervous diseases. By then, the riddle of these unexplainable illnesses —and with it the whole mystery of the human mind—had become the burning interest of his life.

CHAPTER EIGHT

The Strange Case of Anna O.

The people of Vienna liked to think of their city as a cosmopolitan center, and they were justly proud of its music, gaiety, and world-famous coffeehouses. With all that, however, the atmosphere in Vienna was very much like that of a small town where everybody knows a great deal about everybody else, and everybody talks about what he knows.

Freud's gradual shift from the study of brain anatomy to the field of nervous diseases did not go unnoticed in Viennese medical circles. In pompous tones, doctors and professors spoke of his foolishness in leaving a highly admired field for a vague, barely respected one. With equal disapproval their wives clucked their tongues over the lot of Mrs. Freud, bound to a man who seemed to be skidding downhill.

Of all his professors and colleagues at the university, there was only one person whom Freud knew he could count on for support. To him the young man now turned for friendship and understanding.

That man was Joseph Breuer. Freud had met him during the 1870's at Brücke's Institute of Physiology, and the two had formed a deep friendship. Fourteen years older than Freud, Breuer treated him like a son. During Freud's most poverty-stricken days, Breuer continually lent him money, and accepted payments only when he was sure Freud could afford them.

Breuer had a thriving medical practice and was considered one of the finest physicians in Vienna. During the course of his work he had become interested in the use of hypnotism for treating hysterical patients, and he had accidentally made a remarkable discovery.

One of Breuer's very first hysterical patients was a brilliant and attractive twenty-one-year-old girl whom Breuer referred to as Anna O. (In writing and talking about their cases, physicians often use made-up names so as not to betray intimate secrets of the patients' lives.) Anna had cared for her father day and night during his final illness. As the illness progressed, she had developed a whole array of hysterical symptoms, which became worse after he died.

Anna could not move her right arm, although there was nothing physically wrong with it. She constantly coughed, although she had no chest illness. She had double vision, although her eyes were in perfect condition.

Then, too, Anna seemed to suffer terribly. Every afternoon she would fall into a deep sleep—more like a stupor than normal sleep—that would last until about an hour after sunset. Then she would toss and turn miserably, and wake up crying out the words, "To torment! To torment!"

The girl often behaved so weirdly that Breuer did not quite know what to make of her. In the daytime she would suddenly take on a new personality. Instead of the sensitive, intelligent young lady everyone had always known her to be, she became a naughty, spoiled child. She would shout, throw pillows, and have violent temper tantrums. In the evening after her long sleep, however, her old personality would return.

Perhaps the strangest symptom Anna developed was a sudden inability to speak her native German. As a child, she had learned English from her governess, and now, without even realizing it, she spoke only in that language. She could not even understand when people spoke to her in German.

Soon after Breuer began seeing Anna, a startling development took place. During her afternoon stupor she would begin talking to him and telling him "stories." The plot of these stories always centered around a girl keeping watch at her father's deathbed—obviously Anna herself. In her tales, Anna would describe with great accuracy how the "girl" had first experienced a particular symptom. To the amazement of both Breuer and his patient, the very symptom described in the story would disappear when Anna woke up.

Thrilled with these unexpected results, Breuer began hypnotizing Anna every morning to supplement her afternoon talk sessions. At their meetings he would lead her to describe the beginning of each symptom from which she suffered. Although in her waking state the girl could remember none of the events she described to

Breuer, under hypnosis she remembered the most exacting details of how her symptoms had begun.

Anna remembered how she had sat at her father's bedside one afternoon, trying to hold back her tears as she watched her beloved papa growing weaker. Suddenly her father had asked her the time, but she could barely see her watch because of her tear-filled eyes. Soon after that, she began to see double.

She remembered how she had overheard dance music coming from a neighbor's house one evening when she was at her father's side. For a moment she had wished that she could leave the dying man and join the fun next door, but then she immediately reproached herself for that "evil" thought. She had coughed slightly while listening to the music, and ever after had suffered an uncontrollable cough—especially when she heard music playing.

She remembered how she had been frightened once during her father's illness and had wished to pray, but because of her anxiety could think of nothing at the moment but an English nursery rhyme her governess had taught her. Later, she could speak only English.

And so on. Every time Anna remembered the beginning of a symptom and talked about it, the symptom disappeared. The delighted young woman called the method she and Breuer had hit upon the "talking cure," and sometimes she jokingly referred to it as "chimney sweeping" because she swept away the layers of "soot" covering her hidden memories. Breuer named the method "catharsis," after a Greek word meaning "to cleanse." It was, he said, as though the patient felt clean and good after reliving the unhappy experiences that had brought on her symptoms.

Breuer first described this astonishing case to Freud in 1882, long before Freud had learned about hypnotism from Charcot. When Freud went to Paris in 1885 he mentioned Breuer's cathartic method to Charcot, but the Frenchman was too busy with his own experiments to pay much attention to it.

After Freud returned from Paris and had launched into the treatment of nervous diseases himself, he thought a great deal about Breuer's "talking cure," and questioned his friend over and over about the case of Anna O. What had happened to Anna? When had Breuer stopped treating her? Had all her symptoms disappeared? Most important, why had Breuer not published this remarkable case study and shared his findings with other physicians?

Each time that Freud brought up the case of Anna, Breuer seemed embarrassed and reluctant to discuss it. Only after much questioning and pressure was Freud finally able to learn the end of Breuer's story.

Anna continued to grow well as her treatment with Breuer progressed, but she also became very much attached to the physician who had relieved her of so many symptoms. He, in turn, was so intrigued by this case that he devoted more time to Anna than to any of his other patients.

In fact, Breuer spent so much time with Anna that even his wife, whom he loved dearly, began to grow jealous. Suddenly realizing that he had become too caught up in the case, Breuer announced to Anna—with no warning at all—that her treatment was complete and he would no longer come to see her. The girl seemed to accept his decision, and bade him good-bye.

But that very evening Anna's mother frantically fetched Breuer back to the house. Anna was in dreadful pain. She had now developed the strangest symptom of all. The girl believed that she was giving birth to a baby, and worse, that the baby was Breuer's. Through all the months of treatment, Anna had come to think she was in love with Breuer, and to regard him as a husband or sweetheart. His abrupt leave-taking had shocked her into her desperate new symptom.

Horrified at Anna's reaction, Breuer calmed her down with hypnosis, and then left the house for good. Many of Anna's old symptoms returned later and she remained mentally ill for many years, but the prim and proper Breuer would have nothing more to do with her.

The strange case of Anna O. made a profound impression on Freud. Once and for all, it proved something he had been convinced of for a long time: physical matters have nothing to do with the cause of hysteria. The fact that Anna could "talk away" her symptoms showed that they stemmed from emotional experiences—from events that influenced her feelings so deeply that somehow physical symptoms developed.

How an event or feeling from the past can cause an illness, Freud still did not understand. And the unexpected ending of Breuer's tale left him completely puzzled. Why would a highly respectable girl, almost cured of her illness, become so attached to a married man? Why had her attachment so frightened Breuer? Why had her symptoms returned when Breuer stopped treating her?

For the time being, Freud could not solve the many questions left unanswered in the case of Anna O., but he knew that when he did find the solution, it would be an important key to understanding and treating all nervous diseases.

CHAPTER NINE

The Discovery of Psychoanalysis

In his own practice, Freud daily saw patients whose hysterical symptoms could easily match those of Anna O. There was the proper English governess, Miss Lucie, who constantly had the sensation of smelling burning pastry. There was Miss Elisabeth who suffered such severe pains in her legs that she could barely walk. There was Mrs. Emmy von N. who, every few minutes, would break off her conversation with the words, "Keep quiet—don't speak—don't touch me!" There were many other neurotics, as these nervous patients were called, who jammed Freud's consulting room, seeking some relief from their miserable ailments.

But, Freud worried constantly, how could he help these poor creatures when he himself felt so helpless? Unlike physicians who treated "real" physical illnesses, he had few tools available to him.

When he first started his medical practice in 1886, Freud felt duty bound to try out for himself traditional methods of treatment recommended by more experienced physicians. A Professor Wilhelm Erb had written a highly respected textbook showing how electricity can be used in treating nervous patients. So young Freud obligingly bought the complicated electrical equipment necessary for treatment and set out to follow the professor's instructions.

That experiment did not last long. Within a few months, Freud had to admit that all his glamorous new equipment was useless. As for Professor Erb, his textbook, said Freud, "had no more relation to reality than some Egyptian dream book, as is sold in cheap bookstores."

Next, Freud turned to hypnotism. Following Charcot's method of hypnotic suggestion, Freud put his patients into a deep trance. Then he suggested over and over that when the patient awoke, his symptoms would be gone. In many cases, Freud's hypnotic suggestions brought about the desired results, and the patient felt well upon awakening. But as often as not, the patient's good feeling wore off after a while, and his symptoms returned, as violent as they had been at the start.

For Freud, Breuer's exciting method of catharsis soon replaced Charcot's technique of suggestion. Here, certainly, was a real breakthrough in helping nervous patients. For the first time, the physician did not just treat a symptom; he also learned something about the cause of that symptom. Moreover, the results seemed far more permanent than those achieved with hypnotic suggestion.

Still, Freud was not satisfied. Breuer's method, like Charcot's, depended on hypnotism, and the restless young physician was becoming discouraged with hypnotism. In the first place, there were many patients who did not respond to hypnotism. Besides, even with good subjects who could be hypnotized easily, the process was time-consuming and artificial. It involved putting the patient into his trancelike sleep, questioning him about his illness, awakening him, and then starting the whole routine over again at the next session. In addition to everything else, it was a downright bore for both patient and physician.

Surely, Freud reasoned, if a patient can remember forgotten experiences and feelings while he is under hypnosis, those memories must be buried somewhere in his mind. If he tries hard enough, he should be able to produce the same thoughts and memories without hypnosis.

A simple idea—so simple, in fact, it seems hard to believe that this idea led Freud to some of his greatest discoveries. Yet, using it as a starting point, between 1892 and 1896 Freud gradually abandoned hypnotism in treating nervous patients and developed the basic principles upon which the entire practice of psychoanalysis rests.

It was poor, pained Miss Elisabeth who pointed the way. Elisabeth just did not take to hypnotism. Yet Freud knew that the only way she would find relief from the terrible pains in her legs was to talk out the events that had led up to those pains.

One day Freud asked Miss Elisabeth to lie down on the couch in his office, shut her eyes, and concentrate as hard as she could on remembering how her symptoms began. At first she was puzzled, and objected that she could remember nothing. To help her, Freud gently placed his hands on her forehead. Then he assured her that a picture would flash through her mind—a key picture of some event in her past that would lead her to remember the beginning of her illness.

Slowly, very slowly, Miss Elisabeth began to remember. Without hypnotism, without outside influence, just through her own concentration, she began to "see" events of the past in her mind, and in a halting voice to relate them to Freud. As time went on, using this "concentration technique," Miss Elisabeth produced more and more pictures in her mind, as though, said Freud, she was reading "from a large picture book." Just as in hypnosis, talking about events of the past made her feel better.

Elated with his freedom from hypnotism, Freud began to use his new technique with other patients. With each one he followed the same procedure. The patient would lie comfortably on Freud's office couch, and with his hands on the patient's forehead, Freud would urge him to think about his illness. Gradually, by coaxing and encouragement, the patient would remember experiences that might have led to his symptoms—experiences that the patient did not even realize he remembered until he started thinking about them.

Now Freud made another discovery. When left on their own to trace back their memories, many patients did not stop at the "traumatic event," the particular incident that had led to the appearance of a symptom. As the patient talked, one thought led to another until his mind began to travel much farther back. Back it went, back, back, deep into the early days of his childhood.

It was like digging for a buried city. By concentrating and talking, the patient dug up layer upon layer of memories until he reached the very earliest memories of his life, the very core of his being. There, in his childhood, in his first relationships to parents and relatives, he uncovered feelings and wishes that had later developed into painful mental illnesses.

His patient's mental travels back into early childhood soon taught Freud something he had not understood before. A patient's present illness, he now realized, must be dealt with as only one part of a large chain of events going back to that patient's earliest days. Thus Miss Elisabeth's leg pains, or Anna's double vision, might have been triggered off by specific events. But the "why" of the patients' symptoms—the reasons they reacted to those events by becoming ill—these factors could be understood only by going back into their childhood and learning how other emotional events had affected their lives.

With this new insight, Freud never discouraged his patients when their minds wandered from the present or their thoughts seemed to ramble on. Instead, he encouraged them to say whatever came into their heads. He knew that in his own way the patient would eventually uncover the deepest layers of his mind.

Freud made up a special name for his technique of allowing patients to let their minds wander freely back and forth from past to present and from thought to thought. He called it "free association." In 1896, in a monograph, he introduced for the first time the term "psychoanalysis" to describe his method of studying the workings of the mind, using free association as his major tool. The name was built on the Greek word "psyche," which means "soul" or "mind." Psychoanalysis is the analysis of the mind.

With time, Freud improved on his technique of free association. Gradually he stopped touching the patient's forehead or even coaxing him in his memories. Freud assured his patients that they could speak about any idea they thought of, even if the idea seemed silly or improper. He even arranged his chair in such a way that the patient would not have to face him while revealing hidden thoughts.

Even with complete freedom and the most comfortable conditions possible, however, Freud realized that the process of remembering events of the past was a long and difficult one for his patients. He also noticed a curious thing. The very memories and thoughts that turned out to be the key to a patient's illness were often the last to be spoken about. As Freud put it, the patient "resisted" bringing painful feelings and thoughts out into the open even when he was well aware of them. Thus, as it turned out, at the root of Miss Elisabeth's pains lay her secret love for her dead sister's husband—a love she considered immoral. Yet week after week she avoided the subject of her brother-in-law. She spoke about her father, her sister, her mother—everyone but the essential young man.

Connected with this idea of resistance was a far more important discovery that Freud called the theory of repression. In many cases the most crucial thoughts of all in bringing on a patient's illness, Freud observed, were those that even the patient himself had no inkling of.

These were thoughts, emotions, and wishes that the patient had found so painful or bad to begin with that he never dared allow himself to think them through. He had quickly "repressed," or buried, them, said Freud, so that he would not have to face up to them.

The problem with a repressed thought was that it never really disappeared. It lay hidden deep in a person's mind. Years later, some powerful event in the person's life might reactivate this same hidden thought or feeling. Even then, however, it did not dare come forward in its original form. Instead, it was "converted," or transformed, into a nagging symptom.

It could take weeks or months or even years for a patient to dig up the unhappy thoughts and emotions he had repressed. He might have to go through difficult sessions of psychoanalysis in which he relived unpleasant experiences that had led to his repressions. But only then, Freud saw clearly, only when the patient was able to bring his repressed thoughts to the surface and face them squarely, could he be cured.

And what were these terrible feelings and thoughts that Freud's patients had so desperately buried in their minds? Freud's answer shocked all Vienna. These thoughts almost always had to do with matters of love and sex, said Freud. They were connected with intimate relationships between a man and a woman, a husband and a wife, or a child and one of his parents. For the most part, a wish or idea that a patient repressed was one that he was dreadfully ashamed of. That was why it became hidden away. That was why it was so painful to dig up.

Freud's far-reaching theory of repression and his technique of free association became the foundation for his practice of psychoanalysis. There was one more idea that he developed during these fruitful years from 1892 to 1896. That was the idea of transference.

"Transference" was the term Freud used to describe the relationship a patient develops toward his psychoanalyst. As the patient tells his doctor more and more about his past and about his most secret thoughts he becomes more and more attached to that doctor. He begins to transfer to the psychoanalyst the feelings he has had toward other persons in his life. Sometimes he transfers to the doctor feelings he has had toward his father or his brother; at other times the patient regards the doctor more as a close friend or, in the case of a woman, as a sweetheart.

There is nothing wrong with the process of transference. In fact, claimed Freud, it is an essential part of the cure. Because of it the patient feels close enough to his psychoanalyst to discuss the many forbidden subjects he has hidden in his memory. And the transference is not permanent. Once the patient begins to recover from his illness, he becomes less attached to the doctor, and gradually goes back to a more normal relationship with him.

Now that he had thought out the theory of transference, Freud finally understood the mysterious ending of Anna O.'s case. Anna had "fallen in love" with Breuer as part of the transference process, because he was the first person to listen to her and help her. She had done nothing immoral and meant no harm. Had Breuer not been so terribly proper, and had he continued to treat her, Freud realized sadly, she might have become well and happy and found a husband of her own whom she could truly love.

As Freud's startling new ideas developed—almost tumbling one on top of the other during these years—he published short monographs or articles about them in scientific journals. But, daring as he was in thought, he felt a bit timid about gathering his ideas together into a book of his own. Because Breuer's "talking out" method of catharsis had been Freud's starting point, he invited Breuer to join him in publishing their findings. For a long time Breuer hesitated, still shocked and embarrassed by the strange turn Anna's case had taken. In the end he had to give in to Freud's persuasive arguments.

Their joint book, *Studies in Hysteria*, appeared in 1895. It included Breuer's case of Anna O. (with no mention of the final, upsetting incident) and four case studies by Freud. In these studies and in a closing essay, Freud outlined some of his techniques and theories. He also mentioned his growing belief that problems of love and sex lie at the basis of many nervous disorders.

The book—especially, Freud's radical ideas—was badly received by both critics and public. Much worse for Freud, this book marked the end of his friendship with Breuer. The older man had enthusiastically encouraged Freud's investigations into psychoanalysis, but he was too much the Victorian gentleman to accept Freud's emphasis on sexual matters. The two could no longer understand each other or work together.

At the age of forty, Freud was left to carry on his work alone. His best friend had deserted him, his colleagues scorned his theories, and his medical practice declined as scandalous rumors about his ideas spread throughout the city.

Freud never turned back, however. Instead, he began to apply his theory of repression and his technique of free association not only to cases of hysteria, but to many other neurotic patients as well. Some were patients who suffered from terrifying fears; others struggled with uncontrollable anxieties. All responded to Freud's psychoanalytic treatment as they had never responded to electricity and other "cures" imposed on them by the doctors of Vienna.

Opposition to his ideas made Freud more determined than ever to continue his investigations into the deepest thoughts of men's minds. "They regard me rather as a monomaniac," he wrote a friend, "while I have the distinct feeling that I have touched on one of the great secrets of nature."

CHAPTER TEN

Dreams Have Meaning, Too

The year 1896 was a landmark in the life of Sigmund Freud. In October of that year his father died at the age of eighty-one. Jakob Freud had been ill for a long time. Yet when the feeble old man finally passed away, Freud experienced an unexpected, overwhelming grief. In a letter to a dear friend he wrote, "I feel now as if I had been torn up by the roots."

Suddenly memories of his childhood and of the feelings and thoughts he had had about his father began to flood Freud's mind. For months he brooded about those memories. Then in July, 1897, just nine months after his father's death, Freud began the most difficult undertaking of his life: his psychoanalysis of himself. He had come to realize that past events and forgotten feelings had played as important a part in his life as they had in the lives of his patients. Now it was time to turn inward, to explore the thoughts and wishes he had long ago buried deep within himself. Only through self-understanding could he ever completely understand and help the people he treated.

Determined to spare himself no pain or humiliation in

accomplishing his goal, Freud began his challenging task. In doing so, he suffered difficulties that his patients had never experienced during their psychoanalysis. Freud had no one with whom he could talk out his thoughts and memories. There was no one to listen sympathetically or reassure him. All alone he forced his mind to look farther and farther back into the past. All alone he discovered memories and feelings he did not fully understand. Sometimes the memories were so painful that thinking them through left him exhausted, drained of all energy. At other times the memories were sweet and pleasant.

The chief method Freud used to psychoanalyze himself was as unusual as the whole idea of self-analysis. He spent hour after hour studying his dreams as a way of remembering and understanding his innermost thoughts.

The study of dreams, Freud knew, had been practiced as far back as ancient times. The Bible tells the story of how Joseph won a high post as an adviser to the pharaoh of Egypt by interpreting the pharaoh's dreams. In ancient Greece, too, prophets and prophetesses interpreted dreams as a method of foretelling the future. But nobody before Freud had ever attempted to make a scientific study of dreams. Certainly no scientist or scholar in Freud's day took dreams seriously; anybody who did would be regarded as superstitious and foolish.

Freud had a theory about dreams. He had developed it gradually over the years as he saw more and more patients. In fact, he had accumulated a file of over a thousand dreams that his patients had told him during the course of their treatment. To explain how dreams are important, Freud described the human mind as being made up of two parts: (1) the conscious mind, and (2) the unconscious mind.

The conscious mind, Freud said, contains the thoughts and ideas we are aware of when we wake up, go to school, work, eat, play, and think. The unconscious mind contains the thoughts, instincts, wishes, and memories we have repressed and hidden away. The thoughts in our unconscious mind influence our lives just as much as those in our conscious mind, but we are not aware of that influence.

Dreams are a way for the unconscious mind to speak, said Freud. During our waking hours our conscious mind keeps strict control over our ideas and feelings so that none of the forbidden thoughts that we are ashamed of and that we want to keep repressed come forward to disturb us.

When we sleep, our conscious mind relaxes. Then thoughts buried in our unconscious mind come to the surface in the form of dreams. The dreams serve as wish fulfillments. In them we carry out wishes and actions that we do not dare think about in our waking hours. But because our conscious mind never loses complete control, even in our dreams, the repressed thoughts are camouflaged and distorted so that they seem to be mixed up and senseless.

By studying the seemingly mixed-up patterns and images in our dreams, we can learn to interpret those dreams, Freud maintained. Through these interpretations we can come to understand our unconscious mind. Like free association, our dreams can then stir up memories and wishes that we hid away from our conscious mind.

To understand his dreams, Freud trained himself to make detailed notes of them as soon as he awoke each morning. Later in the day he would study these notes carefully. Gradually Freud learned to unravel the confused images and symbols that had appeared in the dreams. Then slowly he was able to discover the thoughts and desires he had repressed and to trace them back to childhood.

Through his analysis of his dreams, Freud remembered that first frightening train trip he had taken as a child when he had left Freiberg with his family. For many years he had felt an unreasoning fear of trains. Only now, when he uncovered the memory of that early trip and understood the reasons for his childhood terror, was he able to conquer his adult fear.

Long-buried thoughts of which he was deeply ashamed also came to light under the glare of Freud's self-analysis. He discovered, for example, that he had been fiercely jealous of his baby brother Julius, who was born when Freud was less than a year old. Freud had resented sharing his mother's love with this newcomer and had secretly wished that Julius would somehow go away. Later, Julius died at the age of eight months. Freud now realized that he had felt a deep sense of guilt after his brother's death, as though he were responsible for it because of the bad thoughts he had had about the baby. That vague burden of guilt had remained with him in his adult life.

Freud even remembered the great attachment he had felt toward his mother, who always treated him as her favorite. Because of that attachment, he saw clearly for the first time, he still paid more attention to his mother than to his wife. He brought his mother flowers every Sunday when he visited her, although he rarely remembered to buy candy or flowers for his wife.

Toward his father, Freud came to understand that he had felt mixed emotions of love and hatred. Through his analysis he recalled one of the few times when the gentle Jakob had lost his temper. As a child of seven or eight years old, Freud had misbehaved and Jakob had exclaimed angrily, "That boy will never amount to anything." After that, almost all the achievements in Freud's life, he realized, were directed at showing his father time and again that he *had* amounted to something, after all.

As his study of dreams and his analysis of himself moved along, Freud told his friends and family that he was like an explorer opening up a dark continent. Every day he pushed deeper and deeper into his unconscious mind, unearthing layers of memories that his conscious mind had known nothing about. Within himself, he confided to a friend, was a "seething ferment."

By 1899, after two years of difficult, almost torturous self-analysis, Freud was ready to publish a book about his experiences and discoveries. The book, *The Interpretation of Dreams*, appeared in 1900. Freud always considered it his greatest work, containing, he said later, "the most valuable of all the discoveries it has been my good fortune to make." All the writings he published during the remainder of his life were elaborations of ideas first presented in this book.

In the book, Freud explained his method of interpreting dreams, and discussed his theories of the conscious and unconscious. Using examples from his own life, he showed how the unconscious influences the behavior of *every* person, not just the mentally disturbed. A mentally ill patient, Freud had become convinced, represents a more extreme example of processes that occur in all people. By using himself to study those processes he was laying the "foundation for a new and deeper science of the mind," which would lead to an understanding of normal as well as abnormal human behavior.

Freud's decision to present his own dreams and his interpretations of them was a difficult one to make. Sensitive and somewhat withdrawn by nature, he suffered at exposing his innermost thoughts to an audience, and revealing, for all to see, his most personal relationships. A proud man, he also found it hard to cast himself in a poor light, as he sometimes had to in this book, showing that he was overambitious and often selfish. But Freud sincerely believed that his ideas and discoveries were too important to be stifled by pride and self-love.

In one part of the book, Freud presented, almost as an aside, a theory of childhood that he had arrived at through his exacting self-analysis. That theory became the most shocking and controversial part of his work. The strong attachment he had felt toward his mother, Freud said, was typical of all little boys. This attachment, he maintained, leads to feelings of jealousy and even hatred toward the father, whom a little boy sees as a rival for his mother's love.

Because children know that it is not "right" to dislike or envy a parent, boys repress their angry feelings toward their fathers. In time, as they grow up and come to meet and love people outside their immediate family, their feelings toward both parents change. But in some men the early conflicts of love for the mother and hatred of the father are never resolved. These conflicts and the repressed thoughts that go with them appear later as mental disturbances that may distort the person's relationships to both men and women.

Freud called the attachment of little boys to their mothers the Oedipus complex. The name came from Oedipus, the hero of an ancient Greek drama, who unknowingly killed his father and married his mother. In later years, Freud developed a similar theory about little girls, who, he said, experience anger and hostility toward their mothers while they "fall in love" with their fathers.

To a public already suspicious of Freud and his unconventional ideas about human thoughts and behavior, *The Interpretation of Dreams* served only to confirm previously held opinions. People began to speak in whispers about "poor" Mrs. Freud whose husband had abandoned a brilliant scientific career and turned into "a rather disgusting freak."

Freud's revolutionary theories about the conscious and unconscious were ridiculed or ignored. His emphasis on dreams and his technique of dream analysis were scoffed at. The greatest criticism of all, though, was reserved for his thoughts about childhood, particularly his idea of the Oedipus complex.

Victorian ladies and gentlemen regarded childhood as an age of innocence. Children just did not experience the feelings of love and hatred that adults had. And the very idea of a little boy loving his mother to such an extent that he hated his father was vulgar and indecent!

When Freud's book appeared, not one scientific journal in Vienna bothered to review it. The few general-interest or literary journals that did mention it had nothing but contempt for Freud's ideas. One assistant at the Psychiatric Clinic in Vienna went so far as to publish a book disproving Freud's theories about dreams without ever having read *The Interpretation of Dreams*. Freud's book, his colleagues assured him, was not worth the bother of reading.

It took eight years for the original six hundred copies of Freud's *The Interpretation of Dreams* to be sold. For his effort, Freud received only about $200. In addition, as a result of the book, his medical practice—already failing because of his previous publications—shrank even more. Freud's reaction to the criticism and insults was simple: he ignored them and kept on working. Still, after the excitement and mental anguish he had gone through in preparing his masterpiece, he could not help feeling bitter and discouraged.

"I have been as good as cut off from the outside world," he wrote sadly in a letter, "not a leaf has stirred to show the interpretation of dreams means anything to anyone."

CHAPTER ELEVEN

Friends and Enemies

The years of self-analysis and the labor of writing *The Interpretation of Dreams* left a lasting mark on Sigmund Freud. By the time the book was published in 1900, no trace remained of the hesitant young man who had cautiously given up medical research to study the unknown field of nervous diseases.

At the age of forty-four, Freud was totally dedicated to investigating the "unexplored regions of the mind" and was proud to claim that he was "the first mortal to set foot" in those regions. Now he could honestly say of himself, "I am not really a man of science . . . I am nothing but by temperament a *conquistador*—an adventurer . . . with the curiosity, the boldness, and the tenacity that belongs to that type of being."

In appearance, too, Freud had changed. His black beard was peppered with gray, and his piercing dark eyes had taken on a new look. It was a stern look, a look almost of anger, with which Freud carefully studied patients and visitors. But the look was softened by a warm smile that seemed always to play around Freud's lips and by a rich voice that managed to add a note of humor to even the most somber situations.

77

By 1900, Freud was also coming to the end of the deepest and strangest friendship of his life. That was his friendship with a physician named Wilhelm Fliess.

Freud had met Fliess in 1887 through his friend Josef Breuer. Two years younger than Freud, Fliess was a highly successful physician in Berlin. He specialized in treating nose and throat ailments, but his scientific interests extended far beyond his medical practice.

Over the years, Fliess had developed an odd, mystical theory about numbers. He believed that each person's life ran in cycles of 23 or 28 days, or various combinations of those numbers. By following the cycles of a person's life one could determine when that person would be ill, when he would marry, when he would die, and so on.

It was almost a magical theory, and one that Freud never really accepted. Fliess was a brilliant and persuasive man, however, and his attractive personality and unusual ideas captured Freud's imagination and held him in their spell. For a long time, Freud even believed that he would die at the age of fifty-one, the age Fliess had predicted for him.

Soon after their first meeting, Freud and Fliess began exchanging casual letters. Gradually, as Freud's friendship with Breuer came to an end, he became more and more attached to Fliess. His letters grew longer and more intimate. With Fliess he discussed politics, literature, and science, and to Fliess he poured out his deepest and most private thoughts as he developed the most important theories of his career.

During the difficult years of his self-analysis, Freud came to regard Fliess almost as a patient might regard a psychoanalyst to whom he was opening his mind. Instead of lying on a couch and talking to him, Freud used pen and paper to describe in long letters to Fliess the dreams he had and the disturbing memories he was uncovering.

Because both men were busy with their medical work —Freud in Vienna and Fliess in Berlin—they had little chance to see each other. Every summer, though, they set aside a few days for a vacation together—just the two of them, without their families.

At these "Congresses," as Freud called them, the two discussed their ideas for hours on end. Fliess, alone among medical men, sympathized with Freud and encouraged him in his theories. Delighted to have such a responsive audience, Freud wrote his friend: "After each of our Congresses I have been newly fortified for weeks, new ideas pressed forward, pleasure in the hard work was restored, and the flickering hope of finding one's way through the jungle burned for a while steadily and brilliantly. . . ."

Then, as suddenly as it had blossomed, the friendship between Freud and Fliess came to an end. During their "Congress" in 1900 the two quarreled about their ideas. Freud criticized some theory of Fliess's. In turn, Fliess accused Freud of being a "thought-reader" and of reading his own thoughts into those of his patients.

They parted bitter enemies. Although Freud later tried to bring about a reconciliation, the two men never met again. Their correspondence gradually broke down, and

came to a final end in 1902. Fliess, like Breuer before
him, had continued the pattern of "intimate friend" and
"hated enemy" that had begun so many years earlier in
Freud's first friendship with his nephew John.

By the time the friendship ended, Freud had come a
long way in his self-analysis. He had gained new understanding of himself, and in many ways was happy to have
broken free of Fliess. He knew that he could go on in his
explorations alone and that he no longer needed to lean
on Fliess for comfort and support.

In spite of this understanding, however, the strong
friendship and abrupt ending left a permanent scar on
Freud. Years later he visited Munich, a German city
he had first seen with Fliess. After lunch at the Park
Hotel with some of his colleagues, he suddenly fell to
the ground, unconscious. After he recovered he explained
that he had been overwhelmed by the strong memory of
Fliess and the time they had spent together in that city
and in that very hotel.

Soon after their friendship ended, Freud destroyed all
the letters he had received from Fliess, and rarely spoke
of his former friend. Until after Freud's death, few persons besides his wife and family knew of his correspondence with Fliess or the depth of their friendship.

The story of how that friendship became known to the
world is a story of intrigue and drama. Unlike Freud,
Fliess had kept the 284 letters he had received from his
friend. After Fliess's death in 1928, his widow sold the
letters to a bookdealer in Berlin. She made the bookdealer promise never to let the letters fall into Freud's

hands, because she knew that he would destroy them.

When the Nazis came to power in Germany during the 1930's the bookdealer smuggled Freud's letters to France. There, Freud's friend Princess Marie Bonaparte bought them for about $500. She later visited Freud in Vienna and told him about the packet of letters. As expected, he furiously demanded that they be burned immediately.

Instead, the Princess deposited her precious papers in a Viennese bank. After the Nazis occupied Vienna, she received permission to remove her valuables from the bank vault. Gestapo officers watched her closely as she lifted the documents from her vault. But they never guessed that the package she handled so carefully contained letters by the Jewish psychoanalyst.

Princess Bonaparte left the letters in the care of the Danish legation in Paris until the end of World War II. Then the letters, wrapped in waterproof material to protect them against a sea disaster, were shipped to London. There, Freud's youngest daughter, Anna, and one of his followers studied them and selected the most important ones for publication.

Had he been alive, Freud would probably have forbidden the publication of such intimate accounts of his thoughts and feelings. Nevertheless, those documents have proved an invaluable guide to understanding Sigmund Freud's teachings. Of all his writings, only those handwritten letters to his one-time friend Wilhelm Fliess describe the suffering, doubts, and triumphs Freud experienced as he arrived at his most daring doctrines.

CHAPTER TWELVE

A Lonely Island

After his breakup with Fliess, Freud could compare himself to Robinson Crusoe living on a lonely island. Now there was no one at all to turn to and nothing at all to look forward to. Intellectually, he lived in almost total isolation, rudely cut off from his former colleagues in Vienna. All he had was his own work and the inescapable truths he must somehow make people understand and accept.

The only way to prove his theories, Freud decided, was to show that they actually worked in practice. So, while treating his patients, he kept careful notes of their problems and progress. Later he published case studies of a number of the patients, describing their symptoms and his treatment of them. As always, in these published case histories, Freud used made-up names for his patients so that nobody would know who they were.

Two of Freud's most famous and controversial case studies were those he called "Dora" and "Little Hans."

Dora was an eighteen-year-old girl whom Freud treated in 1900. When she came to him she suffered from severe attacks of hysteria. She had a wracking nervous cough and would often lose her voice for days on end. Worse, she had become so depressed that she was threatening suicide.

The case of Dora was one of the first in which the psychoanalysis centered around a study of the patient's dreams—in this case, two particular dreams. The dreams revealed to both doctor and patient the deeply repressed thoughts that lay behind Dora's illness. The basis of her problems was, they discovered, a strong attachment to her father—an attachment so fierce and unhealthy that it had caused her to fear and dislike all other men. Her fear of men was aggravated by the situations in which she found herself, and led to many of her hysterical symptoms.

After only eleven weeks of psychoanalysis, Dora suddenly stopped her treatment and never returned to Freud's office. She had become frightened by the forbidden thoughts and wishes her psychoanalysis had uncovered. Freud realized that Dora's treatment had not lasted long enough to cure her of all her problems, but he was pleased to hear several years later that she had married and was able to live a more normal life than she had before. Had she not been treated, he felt, she might have ended by spending her life in a mental institution, or even by taking her own life.

So that nobody in Vienna would recognize the young woman from his description, Freud waited almost five years before publishing the case of Dora. He finally published it in 1905 as a separate pamphlet. In this beautifully written work he revealed that during the course of psychoanalysis he had discussed matters of love and sex with the girl. Without mincing words, he bluntly stated that it is possible for a man to talk about sexual matters with women without harming them, and that, in fact, in the case of a doctor-patient relationship, such a discussion is necessary and desirable.

The furious public reaction to such an outspoken statement did not surprise or even disturb Freud. He felt too satisfied with what he knew was a thorough and important presentation. He even took pride in the writing style, which he had worked over carefully so that the case read more like a fascinating short story than a typically stodgy scientific paper.

In answer to the angry insults hurled at him, Freud commented dryly, ". . . after all, one doesn't write for today only." His words were prophetic. Today, more than sixty years after the publication of the Dora case study, it has become a classic, used as a model by all students of psychoanalysis.

The case of little Hans, which Freud also published during the early 1900's, left him equally pleased with the work he had done and equally condemned from the outside.

Hans was the first young child ever to undergo psychoanalysis. He was only five years old when his parents turned to Freud for help in curing him of a haunting fear he had. The child believed that if he left his house a horse would bite him in the street. As a result of this unreasoning fear of horses he refused to take walks, play with friends, or even step foot outside his own door.

Little Hans's parents were among Freud's very first

followers in Vienna. Because they were highly intelligent
and wished to help their son as much as possible, Freud
set about treating the boy in an unusual way. Hans's
father, rather than Freud, became the child's psychoanalyst.

The father would spend many hours talking to his son
and playing with him in an effort to determine what unconscious problems had led to the boy's uncontrollable
fear of being bitten by a horse. He would then send notes
of his conversations with Hans to Freud, who would ad-
vise him how to proceed. The little boy himself became
so caught up in this "game" that he often reminded his
father to write to the professor who was helping him get
rid of his "nonsense."

Through Hans's play and conversations with his father,
Freud discovered that his fear of horses was related to his
fear of his father. After several months of talking out
many of the thoughts that disturbed him, little Hans recovered from his fears and became a happy, healthy child.
Yet, when Freud published this case study, it, too,
aroused anger and indignation. Freud was criticized for
making such a young child the "victim" of psychoanalysis, and dire predictions were made for the child's future.

The gloomy predictions by the public never came true.
Just the opposite happened. One day many years later,
in 1922, a handsome young man of nineteen presented
himself in Freud's office. The youth shook the doctor's
hand and announced with a warm smile, "I am little
Hans." His psychoanalysis had permitted the once fearful child to develop into a wholesome young man, and

later to become highly successful in his professional life.

Even while Freud devoted most of his time and energy to studying the mentally disturbed during these lonely years he never lost interest in unraveling the mental processes of all men and women. He kept his eyes and ears open to the sights and sounds around him. What he observed—in the prattle of his children, in the gossip of his wife and sister-in-law, in the actions of his friends and neighbors—convinced him over and over of the wide application of his theories.

For in the simple, routine, everyday life of men and women the unconscious mind is constantly at work, Freud saw. Its influence can be clearly recognized, especially in "chance" happenings, in the little forgetful acts and common mistakes that we like to consider accidental.

A gracious lady gushes over a friend's new hat, "I am sure you must have *thrown* this delightful hat together." She meant to say "*sewn*" of course. Why did her tongue slip so that she said "thrown"? Because deep inside, Freud maintained, she really thought the hat looked sloppily thrown together. And, try as she would to hold the unconscious thought back, it pushed its way to the surface, slipping out before she could stop it.

An antiroyalist newspaper prints that "His Highness, the *Clown* Prince," attended a reception. The next day, in apologizing for the error and trying to use the correct words, "*Crown* Prince," the newspaper now refers to His Highness as the "*Crow* Prince." Why? The newspaperman who wrote the story about the Crown Prince has such a strong dislike of royalty that unconsciously he wants to make these errors, although consciously he would not show his feelings in such an unprofessional way.

A young, bossy wife is talking about her husband, who has recently been ill. "The doctor said that diet has nothing to do with his ailments," she tells a friend, "and he can eat and drink whatever *I* want." She mistakenly says, "*I* want," instead of "*he* wants," because unconsciously she even wants to boss her husband's eating habits.

Another young wife, a newlywed, sees her husband strolling down the street. She nudges her companion, saying, "There goes Mr. Snow," forgetting that Mr. Snow has been her husband for several weeks. Could it be that within her unconscious mind she *wants* to forget that Mr. Snow is her husband, or further, wishes he weren't? Her divorce a year later bears out this interpretation.

Freud saw hundreds of similar examples of the unconscious mind at work everyday. In 1904 he gathered many of these examples into a book that he called *The Psychopathology of Everyday Life.* Using delightful anecdotes and serious incidents, he showed just how strongly unconscious desires, thoughts, and memories affect the everyday behavior of all persons.

Surprisingly, to Freud, this book received the best reviews of any of his works when it was published. Later it became one of his most popular writings. Somehow the examples of "accidental" errors that any person can make caught the interest of Freud's readers. It was not long before common slips of the tongue, of the kind that

Freud had explained in his book, became known as "Freudian slips."

But Freud's good reception was short-lived. In 1905, the very next year after his book about everyday errors appeared in print, he published the most shocking of all his works. It was called *Three Essays on the Theory of Sexuality*, and it created a scandal. Where once medical men had been content to ignore or just laugh at Freud's ideas, now they attacked him from all sides, with an intensity that outdid anything he had ever been subjected to.

The book probed those very areas of sensitivity that Freud had merely touched on in his *Interpretation of Dreams:* the question of sexual feelings in children, and especially the Oedipus complex. In no uncertain terms, Freud stated his conviction that children *do* experience feelings of love and sex. They go through very definite phases of development in which sexual matters cannot be ignored, he insisted.

Freud described three phases of development in very young children. In each phase the child has pleasurable sensations that might be compared to sexual feelings, and in each phase these sensations are concentrated on different parts of the body. The phases, according to Freud, are not clear-cut, but overlap one another in time. Freud gave the name "libido" to the generalized sexual energy that expresses itself during these different phases.

In the first phase, during infancy, a baby's mouth is the most important part of the body to him. He gets most of his pleasure through his mouth—pleasure from eating and sucking and even crying. Because the mouth is the center of a baby's feelings in his first phase of development, Freud called this the *oral*, or mouth, phase.

In the next phase, when the child is between two and three years old, he goes through a period of toilet training in which his organs of excretion become important to him. Freud called this second phase the *anal* phase of development.

Freud described the third phase of childhood development in a later edition of his book, and named it the *phallic* phase. In this phase, he said, the child becomes aware of his reproductive organs and of the differences between the sexes. Also during this period of the child's life—when he is about three or four years old—the Oedipus complex begins to develop. Then, little boys become greatly attached to their mothers, and little girls to their fathers.

At about the age of five, Freud explained, the child enters a latency period in which his sexual development is at a standstill. Now he learns to repress the Oedipal feelings he had developed. He learns the meaning of shame, and the moral standards his society expects him to follow. Gradually he buries deep inside himself the impulses and desires to which he had given free rein in the early days of his childhood.

The latency period lasts until about the age of eleven or twelve, when the turbulent adolescent years begin. Often, during early adolescence, an inner struggle takes place between the restrictions the child has developed during the latency period and the reawakened sexual feelings he now begins to experience. But as time goes on, the adolescent boy or girl develops mature sexual feelings that carry him into adulthood.

Men and women who have grown up to live normal, healthy adult lives have passed through the long, complicated process of sexual development smoothly, said Freud. But for many persons the journey is not a smooth one. These persons often become emotionally fixated, or stuck, at one stage or another; and their fixations influence their entire lives.

Thus, a person who is fixated on the oral, or mouth, stage of development may grow up to be a compulsive eater. Always fat, he is always filling his mouth with food and drink. Although he has developed physically, emotionally he has never grown out of the first phase of development when his mouth was the center of greatest pleasure to him. A person emotionally fixated at the stage when the Oedipus complex appeared might retain such a strong and childish love for his mother that he will never find mature love with a woman his own age.

These were some of the main thoughts Freud presented in his most scandalous book. The reaction was instantaneous. "Monster!" "Demon!" "Madman!" people shouted. "He has destroyed forever the innocence of childhood. How could such a man be permitted to practice medicine?"

The insults came steadily, one on top of another. Few persons actually read Freud's book, but everyone talked about it. What he had said soon became so distorted that the very mention of his name was enough to make gentlemen blush and ladies leave the room.

The storm raged around him while Freud quietly continued working in his island of loneliness and isolation. Yet—though he could not be aware of it—his angry critics were waging a losing battle. Even then, in the early years of the 1900's, the seeds of his future fame had been sown. Unnoticed amidst all the uproar, one young man here, another there, had perked up his ears and listened with awe and admiration to the never-before-heard lessons that Sigmund Freud was trying to teach the world.

CHAPTER THIRTEEN

"Herr Professor"

"Congratulations and bouquets keep pouring in," Freud wrote humorously in a letter of 1902, "as if the role of sexuality had been suddenly recognized by His Majesty, the interpretation of dreams confirmed by the Council of Ministers, and the necessity of the psychoanalytic therapy of hysteria carried by a two-thirds majority in Parliament."

The occasion for the congratulations and excitement was Freud's appointment as an Associate Professor at the University of Vienna. Freud had held the lower position of Docent for the unusually long period of seventeen years. His shocking theories, together with strong anti-Jewish feelings among university officials, had barred him from advancement. Time after time his name was passed over while younger and less qualified men received promotions to the rank of professor.

For a long time, Freud had shrugged off the whole matter of a professorship. He had little interest in winning honors. Gradually, however, he had to face the fact that honors were crucial to the snobbish middle-class people of Vienna. A physician could not expect to get by solely on his ability to treat patients. To build a truly successful medical practice in Vienna, he must have an important-sounding title at the university.

Much to his distaste, Freud found himself searching for ways to overcome the prejudice against him and win the title of Professor. Finally one of his patients was able to influence the Minister of Education in his favor. At a solemn ceremony, Freud received his appointment and appeared before the Austrian emperor to offer his thanks.

Almost overnight, Freud noticed a change in attitudes toward him. Acquaintances who, just a few days earlier, had looked the other way when they saw Freud coming, now greeted him with a respectful bow. Colleagues who did not hesitate to publish vicious attacks against his works now felt called upon to write flowery letters of congratulation. Suddenly he was "Herr Professor" Freud, a man with a title—a man to be treated with dignity and honor.

Herr Professor. To Freud the title had little meaning, and the hypocrisy of his countrymen merely made him laugh. He never dreamed that within a few years this title would become known and used with sincere reverence by people throughout the world.

During his long years of loneliness, Freud had no way of knowing that his works were quietly gaining followers in spite of the criticism and abuse they had aroused. He was both amazed and delighted when—beginning in 1902 —a small trickle of visitors appeared at his modest office to seek advice and information.

One of the first to arrive was a black-bearded young

physician named Wilhelm Stekel. During the course of his work with nervous patients he had come across Freud's *Interpretation of Dreams.* So impressed was he with the ideas in the book that he now wished to be psychoanalyzed himself.

Other young men followed Stekel. In 1902, Freud and a few of his newfound followers organized an informal club to discuss psychoanalytic theory and practice. They called themselves the Psychological Wednesday Society. Every Wednesday evening they met in Freud's waiting room on the ground floor of his apartment at Berggasse 19. He and Martha had moved to that apartment in 1891, and there he had carried out his most important work in psychoanalysis.

By 1907 the group had so many members that it had to move to larger quarters in the nearby College of Physicians. In 1908 its name was changed to the Vienna Psycho-Analytical Society.

The men who made up this first band of psychoanalysts had differing backgrounds and interests. There was Stekel, a man of wild imagination and winning personality, who sometimes colored the truth to make a point. There was Alfred Adler, the "ugly duckling" of the group. Short and homely, he did not hesitate to speak his mind even if it meant offending someone else. Then there were Otto Rank and Hanns Sachs, neither with any medical training but both eager to learn the techniques of the new science of psychoanalysis. And there was Karl Abraham, a somewhat stuffy German who had studied psychiatry in Switzerland and then opened a medical practice in Berlin. Always pleasant, always hopeful, he was probably the most stable of Freud's early followers, and he and Freud became close friends.

Beginning in 1906, when Freud was fifty years old, visitors began arriving from many countries to meet him. One of these visitors was a tall, stately, moustached physician in his early thirties. His name was Carl Gustav Jung, and he was a highly respected professor at the Psychiatric Clinic in Zurich, Switzerland. Jung and Freud had corresponded for some months and had arranged to meet for the first time in February, 1907. Later, Jung remembered their meeting this way: "We met at one o'clock in the afternoon and talked virtually without a pause for thirteen hours. Freud was the first man of real importance I had encountered; in my experience up to that time, no one else could compare with him. There was nothing the least trivial in his attitude. I found him extremely intelligent, shrewd, and altogether remarkable."

Almost immediately a very special relationship grew up between Freud and Jung. Pleased by Jung's interest in him, Freud took the bright and thoroughly charming young man into his confidence and treated him like a favored son.

Another foreign visitor who became especially important to Freud was Ernest Jones. A quiet, diligent English doctor, Jones remained throughout his life one of Freud's most loyal followers. During the 1950's he wrote the most comprehensive biography ever published of Freud's life and work.

Many of the young men who gathered around Freud later became famous psychoanalysts in their own right. But in these early years they were somewhat shy with one another and awed by their master, whom they considered a true genius. In speaking to Freud or about him, they never used his name. To them he was always "Herr Professor"—the title he had waited so long to achieve.

Among themselves, Freud's followers loved to exchange amusing anecdotes about the professor. A favorite was the story of the Swiss psychiatrist Max Eitingon. He came to Vienna in 1907 to consult with Freud about one of his patients. To his surprise he found his "consultation" hours taking place during Freud's regular after-dinner walk. Every evening the two would march briskly through the streets of Vienna while Freud talked rapidly about the patient's treatment and poor Eitingon breathlessly tried to keep up with the swift pace and brilliant flow of ideas.

In 1908, at the suggestion of Jung, an international meeting of psychoanalysts was organized. It became the first in a series of International Psycho-Analytical Congresses that are still held today. More than forty persons attended the meeting, which took place on April 26 in Salzburg, Germany. Those present came from many lands—England, Austria, Germany, Hungary, Switzerland, and even far-off America.

As a result of this meeting the first periodical devoted exclusively to psychoanalytic matters was established. Now Freud and his followers no longer had to worry about having their works rejected by unsympathetic scientific journals. They had a journal of their own in which to express their ideas.

After so many years of ridicule, Freud was almost beside himself with happiness at this first congress. He was especially pleased with the admiration and respect shown him by his favorite, Jung. In his joy he did not notice that some of his earliest followers from Vienna were beginning to feel jealous of the attention he gave Jung and the other "foreigners."

In December, 1908, Freud found new cause for happiness. He received an invitation to lecture in the United States at Clark University in Worcester, Massachusetts, on the occasion of the twentieth anniversary of the founding of the university. The invitation was issued by G. Stanley Hall, a distinguished American psychologist, and president of the university. In a flurry of excitement, Freud prepared for the trip, inviting Sandor Ferenczi, one of his followers, to accompany him. Jung had also received an invitation from the university, and the three men arranged to travel together. They set sail for America on August 21, 1909.

To pass the time, and compare techniques, they spent a good part of the six-day sea voyage in analyzing one another's dreams. In New York, where their ship landed, they eagerly visited museums and parks, ate at elegant restaurants—later complaining of indigestion—and attended the first motion picture any of them had ever seen. Then they traveled by train to New England for Freud's talks.

Freud gave five lectures in German on the principles

and aims of psychoanalysis. He spoke swiftly and confidently, without notes. As usual, many newspapers and journals criticized his ideas, but for the first time, he also saw reviews that praised his work. When he was presented with an honorary Doctorate degree at Clark University, Freud was almost overcome with emotion.

"This is the first official recognition of our endeavors," he said softly.

A high point of Freud's trip to the United States was his introduction to the foremost American philosopher of the time, William James. Old and feeble, James had insisted on meeting Freud. After a brief visit together, the philosopher, in a hoarse, barely audible voice, whispered his belief that the future of psychiatry belonged to Freud and his followers.

Years later, in his autobiography, Freud wrote of his trip to the United States, "At that time I was only fifty-three. I felt young and healthy and my short visit to the new world encouraged my self respect in every way. In Europe I felt as though I were despised; but over there I found myself received by the foremost men as an equal."

Still, Freud felt no personal attachment to the United States and never returned there. He found the food too rich, and the informal way of life too different from his own strict, conservative routine.

"America is a mistake," he jokingly confided to a friend. "A gigantic mistake, it is true, but none the less a mistake."

Back home at the end of September, Freud busied himself with his rapidly growing movement. In 1910 an

International Psycho-Analytical Association was formed, and soon individual national societies similar to the one in Vienna began cropping up in countries throughout the world.

Now, however, Freud could no longer close his eyes to the tensions that had appeared during the first international meeting in 1908. One by one, many of his original followers began to break away from the international association and from Freud.

The first to leave was Alfred Adler. Almost from the beginning, Adler had resented the professor's warm friendship with the "foreigner" Jung, especially since he, Adler, had been one of the very first persons to rally to Freud's side. In his outspoken way, Adler made little effort to hide his resentment. In addition, he and Freud had gradually come to a parting of the ways in their thinking. Adler no longer accepted Freud's emphasis on the Oedipus complex, on the unconscious, and on repressions as the basic factors in nervous illnesses. He had a theory of his own, and it stemmed directly from his personal experience.

The small and ugly Adler had suffered extreme feelings of inferiority while he was growing up. To make up for these feelings and for his physical ugliness he had developed his intellect and cultivated a strong personality. Now he believed that a feeling of inferiority—which he called an inferiority complex—is the most important element in shaping all personalities.

In some ways everybody tries to compensate, or make up, for some feeling of inferiority that he has, said Adler.

Each person's behavior and personality stem from the way that person compensates. A fat person may try to be jolly and happy so that people will not think about how fat he is. A short person often acts bossy and aggressive so that he will be noticed in spite of his height. It is this inferiority complex and the compensations that people make for it, more than the Oedipus complex and sexual matters, that should be the main focus of psychoanalysis, Adler insisted.

As Adler became more convinced of his theory he turned more and more against Freud. For his part, Freud considered Adler's views not only "incorrect," but also "dangerous" for the future growth of psychoanalysis. He did not deny the influence of the inferiority complex in shaping personality, but he regarded it as secondary to the far more important influence of the unconscious mind.

It finally became clear that the two men could no longer work together, and in 1911 Adler resigned from the Vienna Psycho-Analytical Society. He and Freud had nothing more to do with each other. Later Adler went to the United States, where he built a highly successful psychiatric practice.

Stekel's resignation followed about a year after Adler's. He, too, resented Freud's interest in foreign psychoanalysts and he, too, wished to develop his own ideas. Specifically, he wanted to shorten the amount of time given to psychoanalysis, allowing each patient only from three to six months. He also believed that the analyst should take an active part in analytic sessions and direct the patient's behavior, instead of allowing the complete freedom Freud had insisted on. Like Adler, Stekel also went later to the United States and won great popularity. But, unlike Adler, he did not become bitter toward Freud. Years after he had left Freud he still spoke of being the professor's "apostle."

For Freud the most painful break of all came in 1913 when his friendship with Jung ended. Jung, his chief confidant, his chosen "heir" as the future leader of psychoanalysis, had finally turned against him, also.

Jung had gradually tried to introduce vast changes into psychoanalysis. What hurt Freud most was that the Swiss psychiatrist had come to deny the importance of early sexual development. That was Freud's most controversial theory and the one whose acceptance he had worked hardest to achieve. Yet, to win public approval, Freud felt convinced, Jung increasingly played down sexual matters in his approach to psychoanalysis. In addition, Jung became less interested in the individual, as time went on, and more interested in a kind of mystical application of psychoanalytic ideas to history and mythology.

As the differences between Freud and Jung grew stronger, their letters became angry and their meetings unpleasant. Freud felt that Jung had nothing more to contribute to psychoanalysis. In turn, Jung accused the professor of having a "personal power drive." By 1912 their friendship had cooled considerably, and it came to an end in 1913. A year later, Jung resigned as president of the International Psycho-Analytical Association to found a movement of his own.

Over the years, others of Freud's original followers broke away from him in much the same way as children often break away from their parents to strike out on their own. Nevertheless, for all the men who left him, many others remained loyal to "Herr Professor." In 1912, five of his most devoted followers, led by Ernest Jones, formed a special group called "the Committee." Its purpose was to help Freud and protect him and his ideas from attack. As a symbol of their friendship, Freud gave each Committee member a ring engraved with an antique Greek head. The group lasted about ten years. Then deaths and disagreements brought it to an end.

The pain and bitterness Freud had felt at the departure of many of his close followers showed themselves in a book called *The History of the Psycho-Analytic Movement*, which he published in 1914. In this book he described in detail the differences between his theories and those of Adler, Jung, and other former colleagues. He tried to show that he cared little about personal power or glory. His only concern was to save from destruction those ideas and principles to which he had devoted his life. This was the only book Freud ever wrote in which he defended himself and his theories.

CHAPTER FOURTEEN

Serving a Tyrant

"How does Professor Freud manage to *do* so much?"

The question arose again and again among Freud's patients and followers. It certainly seemed as though the professor never stopped doing things in order to rest or sleep.

During the very years when he was at his busiest, as his psychoanalytic movement spread and his medical practice began to grow again, Freud extended his explorations further than ever. Now he went beyond the individual to apply his psychoanalytic theory to many areas —literature, religion, art, history. From a psychological point of view, everything interested him. Every day he found new interpretations in fields that once he had considered far removed from psychoanalysis.

On a summer vacation in 1906 he happened to read the novel, *Gradiva*, by the Danish author, Wilhelm Jensen. By 1907 he had published an essay called *Dream and Delusion* in which he showed how the novel's plot reflected the unconscious memories and desires of the author. He even struck up a correspondence with the author who, Freud said, "expressed his pleasure, etc., and declared that the analysis agreed in all important points with the purpose of the story."

Something about a patient he was treating in 1909 reminded Freud of the Italian Renaissance painter Leonardo da Vinci. The psychoanalyst had long been intrigued by the mysterious smile of the famous "Mona Lisa" and of other figures in Leonardo's paintings and drawings. Over the years he had read quite a bit about the artist's life. Now he became intensely interested in Leonardo's genius and personality, and set out to learn as much as he could about the painter. The result of his studies was a psychoanalytical biography of Leonardo da Vinci published in 1910. In the book, Freud suggested the possibility that the smile Leonardo painted over and over again in his works represented the artist's unconscious childhood memory of his own mother's serene smile.

A new book on primitive religion by the anthropologist Sir James Frazer launched Freud into a completely different field in 1910. During the next three years he read just about everything ever written on early religion and mythology. By 1913 he was ready to publish a book of his own on the subject.

Freud's book, *Totem and Taboo*, presented a psychoanalytic approach to primitive religion. In it Freud compared the thinking of early man to the thinking of a child. The Oedipus complex and other psychoanalytic concepts, he said, help us understand primitive beliefs and practices just as they help us understand childhood thoughts and behavior. Through these psychoanalytical interpretations, Freud maintained, we can explain the origins of primitive religion and society.

Art, religion, anthropology—these ventures into new fields excited Freud, but they also brought new criticism on him. At one time he had disturbed only medical people. Now, with each publication, whole groups of specialists quickly rose to refute his theories.

But now, as often as not, the criticism was tempered by respect for the vastness of Freud's interests and knowledge. "How does Professor Freud manage to *do* so much?" his critics echoed the awed question of his admirers.

How indeed? For Freud the answer was clear. "A man like me cannot live without a hobby-horse, a consuming passion . . . a tyrant," he declared. "I have found my tyrant, and in his service I know no limits. My tyrant is psychology."

In the service of his "tyrant," Freud ordered his life in a rigorous routine of work that allowed not a second of wasted time. That routine began precisely at seven o'clock every morning when Freud rose, dressed, ate breakfast, and prepared himself to see his first patient at eight. From eight o'clock to one in the afternoon, Freud treated patients. He devoted exactly fifty-five minutes to his analytical session with each patient, allowing himself five minutes between patients to clear his mind.

At one o'clock in the afternoon the Freud family gathered for a large lunch. His children later recalled that Freud often came to lunch so preoccupied with his work that he barely said a word throughout the entire meal.

Immediately after lunch, Freud took a long walk through the surrounding neighborhood, thrashing out psychoanalytical problems in his mind as he walked briskly along. By three o'clock he was back at work. He continued treating patients steadily until nine in the evening, rarely even stopping for a cup of coffee to relieve himself from the strain of the work. Then the family had supper.

Supper gatherings were more cheerful than the lunches, because by that time Freud was able to relax after his hard day. Afterward he walked again, this time with his wife, his children, or one of his students.

Later, when the rest of the family retired for the night, Freud went to his study There he worked on his many books, went over proofs, and caught up on his correspondence, which grew larger every year. Because he hated the clattering noise of a typewriter, Freud refused to learn how to type, and wrote all his letters and books in longhand.

Oddly, Freud found that he did his best writing when he felt a bit ill. ". . . I have to be somewhat miserable in order to write well," he said. When he felt healthy, he claimed, he was "terribly lazy."

Freud almost never left his study before one or two o'clock in the morning. Still, he managed to appear fresh and alert each day as he greeted his first patient.

Every other Tuesday evening, Freud attended meetings of the B'nai B'rith, a Jewish intellectual club. Every Wednesday evening he joined other psychoanalysts at the regular meeting of the Vienna Psycho-Analytical Society, where he often delivered a paper or lectured to the group. And on Saturday evenings he always played cards with some friends. On Sundays he visited his mother in the morning and took his children to the museum or visited with friends in the afternoon. For eight or nine months of the year these were the only breaks the professor allowed in his daily routine.

In the summertime, however, Freud permitted himself to relax a little. Like others in Vienna, he and his family escaped the unbearable summer heat to spend two or three months in the country. Often they vacationed in the beautiful Austrian Alps, where Freud loved to climb the mountains. Many summers, Freud traveled through Italy with a friend or relative for several weeks before joining his family at their summer resort. Almost always, he continued his writing and began new projects during his summer vacation.

Outside of work Freud's only important interest was his hobby of collecting the figurines and pottery of ancient days. "Those things cheer me and remind me of distant times and countries," he said of the ancient Greek, Roman, and Egyptian sculpture that filled his bookshelves and covered his desk. When he was able to find a piece of sculpture for his collection among the ruins he visited in ancient Rome, it was the high point of a summer vacation.

Day after day and year after year Freud's routine of living remained unchanged. In his logical and methodical way he loved its precise timing. It was the only way he knew to accomplish the many things he still saw ahead of him.

CHAPTER FIFTEEN

In War and Peace

One hot July day in 1914, Freud's routine was shattered. Totally absorbed in his family and his work, the professor had not noticed the black war clouds gathering over Europe. He had not heard the distant rumble of guns or paid attention to the petty quarrels that had risen among the world's nations. To him, as to many of his countrymen, World War I, which began in that summer of 1914, came as a complete surprise.

Later, people called it the Great War or the War to End All Wars, but at first they took it almost lightly. Like others in Vienna, Freud felt convinced that his country was right. In no time at all, he assured Martha and the children, the Central Powers—Austria-Hungary, Germany, Turkey, and Bulgaria—would crush the Allies —Belgium, France, Great Britain, and Russia.

Caught up in the war fever that swept his country, Freud excitedly followed the daily battles and cheered his nation's victories. "I should be with it with all my heart," he announced to friends in discussing the war, "if only I could think England would not be on the wrong side."

The first flush of excitement soon passed, however. There was no quick victory for either side. The days turned into months, and the months into years, and still the war did not end. Over the years, Freud's three sons, Martin, Oliver, and Ernst, enlisted in the Austrian army, and all three were sent to the fighting front. Outwardly the professor showed no emotion as he saw his sons off on their war missions, but through the long years of separation, Freud wrote his boys loving and concerned letters. Like parents in all parts of the world, he reminded them over and over to dress warmly and take care of themselves.

To one of his followers, Freud described with feeling how "our eldest son wrote that a bullet had gone through his cap and another had grazed his arm, neither of which, however, interfered with his activities. . . . Since we don't dare to look into the future, we just live for the day and try to get out of it what it is willing to yield."

As time went on, Freud's practice, which had grown prosperous in the years just before the war, declined dangerously. Money was scarce, and people were too caught up in war activities to think about psychoanalysis. With his consulting room empty and many of his younger colleagues serving in the armed forces, Freud found himself, once again, living a lonely and isolated life.

"I often feel as alone as during the first ten years when I was surrounded by a desert," he complained, "but I was younger then and still endowed with an infinite capacity for holding out."

To make matters worse, he could not even correspond with many of his closest followers who lived in England and Italy, because the war had made them official enemies.

By 1915, Freud no longer spoke of one side or another being "right." The horrors of the war as it spread throughout the world shocked him, and the stories of atrocities on both sides filled him with disgust. This, he decided, was the most "hideous" of all wars. With more insight than that possessed by many persons of his day, he realized that never again would he or his contemporaries recapture the simple joys of prewar times. But he could not know that less than twenty-five years later the world would be swept up in a second war a hundred times more devastating in its effects.

In 1915, in an outburst of pessimism and despair, Freud published a book of two essays called *Thoughts for the Times on War and Death*. In the first essay, "The Disillusionment of the War," he wrote bitterly of the barbaric way in which the nations of the world were slaughtering their people in battle. For all the outward signs of civilization and for all the "progress" nations claimed, Freud maintained, the Western world had not really risen far above primitive cultures. We need not be disillusioned with the evil we see around us, however, he said ironically. People have not really sunk so low as we might imagine; the sad truth is, they never had risen so high, to begin with, as we in the West liked to believe.

Freud called the second essay "Our Attitude to Death." In it he pointed out that nobody ever truly believes that he or his loved ones will die someday. Only a terrible catastrophe such as war makes death seem real. In that sense, the only good that comes from war is that it forces us to value life more than ever.

To pass the time usefully during the bleak winters of 1915 and 1916, Freud gave a series of twenty-eight lectures at the University of Vienna. To his amazement he found students crowding into the lecture hall to hear him speak. Even in narrow-minded Vienna, where he had been rejected for so long, his ideas had begun to win acceptance. Freud published his lectures in 1917 in a book called *Introductory Lectures on Psychoanalysis*. Clearly and simply written, these lectures became a kind of primer of psychoanalysis. They are still considered among the best explanations of Freud's discoveries that have ever been written.

By the time that book of lectures appeared in print, Freud knew that his country had no chance of winning the war. With the United States now in the battle against them, it was just a matter of months before the Central Powers surrendered.

Defeat filled the air in Vienna, and every day the hardships mounted. Lack of oil left homes unheated in a bitter-cold winter. Food shortages grew so severe that even the tiniest piece of meat on the dinner table became a cause for celebration.

Still Freud, now suffering from rheumatism and malnutrition, managed to continue his routine of working and writing as much as possible. Wrapped in his overcoat in his icy study, he wrote, with numbed fingers,

"Curiously enough, with all that I am quite well and my spirits are unshaken. It is a proof of how little justification in reality one needs for inner well-being."

The situation turned worse after the war ended, in 1918, with the defeat of Austria and Germany. As thousands of ragged, half-starved soldiers trooped back from the war front, food shortages mounted. Prices rose to ridiculous heights, and money became almost worthless. In hungry Vienna a slice of bread cost almost as much as a house once had.

Within a short time all of Freud's savings—almost $30,000—were wiped out. At the age of sixty-two the professor was back where he had started, once again haunted by the specter of poverty and faced with the daily torment of finding a way to provide for his large family. Urged by his British friend Ernest Jones, he vaguely considered moving to England. But, for all his intellectual boldness, Freud knew that in everyday life he was too set in his habits to make such a move.

"I will stay at my post as long as I reasonably can," he decided. Twenty years passed before he did leave that post, forced out by Nazi terrorism.

For two years after World War I, Freud struggled to regain the degree of prosperity and comfort he had begun to enjoy before the struggle. He and Martha scrimped and saved to support themselves and help their children, many of whom were now married and raising families of their own.

One day a letter arrived at Berggasse 19, bearing what Freud considered good tidings. His friend Max Eitingon, who had an independent income aside from the money he earned as a psychoanalyst, had written to say that he had sent an order for $780 in Swedish currency to Freud's bank for the professor's use. When Freud read the letter to his family, his sons cheered the news. But his wife and youngest daughter acted hurt and insulted. Did Herr Eitingon suppose that their beloved professor would not be able to see his way to providing for his family without help from the outside?

To himself, Freud had to admit that Eitingon, of course, was right. But to satisfy the pride of the women in his family, he thanked his friend for his generosity and quickly canceled the money order at the bank.

A little later, in desperation, Freud hit on an idea to earn extra money on his own. Why not write a series of articles on psychoanalysis for an American magazine? Magazines always paid well, he reasoned, and his ideas had long enjoyed greater popularity in the United States than in any other country. Immediately he wrote to his nephew, Edward Bernays, who lived in the United States, asking him to arrange the matter. The answer came back that the editors of a well-known woman's magazine would be most interested in having Freud write some articles for them. Their idea was to keep the articles light and lively—nothing stuffy. As first topics they suggested, "The Wife's Mental Place in the Home" and "The Husband's Mental Place in the Home."

The discussion went no further. To a dignified Austrian professor who had devoted his entire life to serious scientific study, such topics were ridiculous and insulting. In a biting letter to the magazine's editor in chief, Freud turned down the offer. Never again did he even think of writing for popular publications.

By the end of 1920, Freud's financial crisis was over. Slowly his practice began to grow again, and day by day his fame spread. Patients arrived from many parts of the world, and paid him in foreign currencies that had not lost their value. His works were translated into almost every language and sold thousands of copies. Perhaps most satisfying to Freud, along with his new prosperity, was the fact that his psychoanalytic movement, interrupted by the war, began to expand rapidly. He and his followers even started an international publishing house devoted strictly to psychoanalytic literature.

Freud had every reason to believe that he had seen his worst days, and that now, at the age of sixty-four, he could look forward to a calm and full old age. That was not to be his fate. For in the up-and-down pattern that had become typical of Freud's entire life, a new series of staggering blows struck swiftly and suddenly, leaving him dazed and shocked from their effect.

The first blow came in 1920, the very year when his income had finally picked up after the war. An epidemic of influenza that had been raging through Europe and killing thousands of persons took its toll in the Freud family. First, Freud's wife fell seriously ill. She had barely recovered when word came that their married daughter Sophie, who lived in Hamburg, was stricken.

Within two days the beautiful, twenty-six-year-old Sophie died. For years during the war, Freud had prepared himself for the possible death of his soldier sons. They had returned safely, but his lovely daughter was gone instead. Numbed by the sudden tragedy, Freud could only say unbelievingly, "She was blown away as if she had never been."

Three years later another blow struck. Sophie's young son, Heinz Rudolf, died of tuberculosis during a visit to Vienna. The boy, whom Freud called "Heinerle," had been his favorite grandchild. His death affected the professor in a way that no other event ever had before or would again—more deeply even than the death of his father years earlier. For the first and only time that anyone could remember, he cried openly.

Freud could not say exactly what it was that made Heinerle so precious to him, but he never quite recovered from the loss of the little boy. Even years later, he could not forget the sweet and delicate grandchild he had so often fondled on his knee. "I don't think I have ever experienced such grief," he told a friend. "I work out of sheer necessity; fundamentally everything has lost its meaning for me."

Freud's inconsolable grief over little Heinerle's death made his own physical suffering seem unimportant. Yet that same year, when he was sixty-seven, he underwent an agonizing operation that was to be the first of thirty-three such ordeals he would suffer during the remainder of his life.

A habitual cigar smoker—he smoked as many as twenty cigars a day—Freud had developed cancer of the mouth. At first his physician and family tried to hide the true nature of his illness from him, but as a well-trained doctor he easily guessed that the awful growth removed from his jaw in April, 1923, was cancerous.

Freud knew that the disease ultimately would be fatal. He did not know that he would suffer its torments for sixteen years. As he underwent successive operations during those years, more and more of his mouth and jaw were cut away. As a result he could barely swallow, and his speech became thick and slurry. Eventually he also grew so deaf in his right ear that he had to change the seating arrangement in his office, so that his patients could speak into his left ear. Often, when the pain became too severe, Freud would sit through an entire analytic session with a hot-water bottle held to his neck.

Soon after his first operation, Freud began wearing a special metal appliance that served as a mechanical jaw. It was an ugly contraption, difficult to insert in his mouth and extremely painful to wear. Freud nicknamed it "the monster." In his most tortured moments he still managed to joke about its ability to dominate his life.

Throughout his illness Freud's only nurse was his youngest daughter, Anna. Martha, of course, watched over her beloved husband, helping him in whatever way she could. But it was delicate Anna, trained as a nurse, who took on the full responsibility for his care. There was an unspoken agreement between Anna and her father: she must treat him professionally, without sentiment or tears, whether she was changing a dressing, helping him insert "the monster," or standing by helplessly as he flinched with pain.

Anna courageously carried out her end of the bargain, and gladly, without complaining, devoted many years of her life to the care of her father. She was the only one of Freud's children who never married. She was also the only one who became a psychoanalyst, achieving fame in her own right for her work with children.

The trials that Freud suffered during the war years and the tragedies that came during the years of peace took their toll of the founder of psychoanalysis. His thick head of hair had thinned considerably and, like his beard, it was filled with white. His body had become frailer, his face more gaunt. But his eyes burned as brightly as ever, and in spite of illness and heartache he carried himself well, with an air of strength and confidence.

Freud had good reason to feel confident, for now, even while he suffered his deepest tragedies, he stood at the threshold of his greatest triumphs of fame and honor.

CHAPTER SIXTEEN

At the Height of Success

The postman who delivered the mail to Berggasse 19 had a difficult life. There was barely a family he could name in all of Vienna who received as much mail as the Freuds. It was bad enough with Frau Professor Freud writing to her mother in Germany and her brother in the United States; and with all those children, when they were living at home, corresponding with friends and relatives. But the professor himself! Neither age nor illness nor hardship ever stopped the flow of his pen or the steady stream of letters that poured into his house every day.

The letters came from all over the globe. From every corner of the earth, people wrote to Professor Freud about their problems; and he, in his thorough manner, answered every letter he received. It did not matter whether he knew the writer or not; a personal letter deserved a personal answer.

So the postman was kept busy, but he was not the only person affected by Freud's ever increasing popularity. So many of the letters Freud received were requests from men and women who wanted to be psychoanalyzed by him that he could not possibly handle all the cases himself. Instead, he constantly referred patients to his fellow analysts in many parts of the world, helping in that way to build their reputations.

Still the requests kept coming. Nearing seventy, an age when most men have long since retired, Freud found himself with more work than ever. "I never realized that the older one grows the more there is to do," Freud told his son Ernst. "Much of my time is taken up with refusals and information to all corners of the world; everyone wants to be analyzed by me. . . ."

The burden of letter writing and the huge case load he carried left the professor with precious little time for his research and writing. Sometimes he looked back almost nostalgically to the lonely years when there was no one to talk to. Unhappy as he had been, at least then he was able to develop his theories without interruption.

There was still so much he wanted to say. During all the years of the 1900's, since he had first made his psychoanalytic discoveries, Freud had never stopped testing and retesting his ideas. As he reviewed old problems and investigated new ones he was not afraid to revise his explanations or to expand his concepts to include the additional observations that arose from his growing experience.

In the few free moments he could snatch during the day and in the late hours of the night, Freud worked over his books, writing footnotes and new introductions to those already in print, and editing and correcting those new ones he was composing. Always a perfectionist, he was rarely satisfied with what he wrote. He could count on his fingers those few works that really pleased him in their presentation: *The Interpretation of Dreams*, the cases of Dora and little Hans, maybe one or two other pieces. For the most part, Freud worried over each book, continually criticizing himself for not doing a better job of explaining his ideas.

One of the most important books he worked on, and finally finished in 1923, was a new study of the mind that supplemented his earlier theories of the conscious and the unconscious. After *The Interpretation of Dreams*, the book became perhaps his most influential psychoanalytic work. It had such a puzzling title, however, that when it first appeared, people wondered what it could possibly mean. It was called *The Ego and the Id*.

Freud had adapted the words "ego" and "id" from the Latin, and used them to describe two parts of man's personality. A third part, also introduced in this book, he called the "superego."

According to Freud, every person possesses within himself deeply buried instincts and drives no different from the savage instincts that dictated the behavior of primitive man hundreds of thousands of years ago. These instincts—greed, lust, desire, hate, as well as love—make up the part of man that Freud called the *id*. They have to do with the "I want" of a person's nature, his desire to satisfy his own selfish needs and wants.

Opposed to the id is the part of man's personality that judges and organizes the untamed instincts and drives he possesses. This part of the mind Freud called the *ego*, or the self. The ego is the "civilized" part of a person, the part that reacts to the world outside himself and channels the impulses of the id so that they do not bring him into conflict with that world.

The *superego*, the third part of man's personality, serves as his conscience. It dictates the do's and don't's that determine his behavior.

Just as sexual development moves through stages, so the id, the ego, and the superego appear at different stages in a person's life. A newborn baby is a mass of uncontrolled and undirected instincts, Freud explained. He has no ego or superego, but simply seeks to fulfill his own desires. He cries when he is hungry, gurgles happily when fed, and sleeps most of the time, unaware of the world outside himself. He is controlled by his id and operates on what Freud called the pleasure principle.

As the child grows a bit older he develops an ego and becomes aware of the real world and his relation to it. He begins to operate on the reality principle, in which he is able to control his own desires in order to meet the demands of the outside world.

At a still later stage, the superego develops as the child learns and accepts his parents' ideas of right and wrong. To satisfy the superego, the ego now represses the forbidden desires and impulses of the id.

In mentally healthy persons the id, ego, and superego work in harmony, giving the person a balanced approach to life that takes into account both his own wants and his responsibilities to society. In some forms of mental illness the ego and the superego are not strong enough to control the drives of the id. Then the person gives himself up to his most primitive instincts, often committing criminal acts as he goes about satisfying his drives. In other cases, mental illness is brought about by an over-demanding superego. Hounded by the superego, the person constantly feels guilty and seeks to punish himself. One role of psychoanalysis, Freud pointed out, is to strengthen the ego so that it can control the instincts of the id on the one hand, and resist overly pressing demands by its "stern master," the superego, on the other.

Freud felt depressed and dissatisfied after he finished writing this important book. He complained that his ideas would appear obscure to his readers. Contrary to his worries and in spite of the new and strange vocabulary in the book, the theories Freud presented were widely accepted. In a short time, "ego," "id," and "superego" became almost household words, used frequently in popular books, magazines, and newspaper articles as well as in professional journals.

It was a strange reversal of roles to have Freud criticizing himself while others praised him—after all those years in which nothing he did seemed to be right. Times had changed, though, and his battle for acceptance was almost over. Now, in the 1920's, the slights and insults he had suffered for so long had begun to fade into the past. In intellectual circles everywhere, people considered it smart and sophisticated to use psychoanalytic terms and to quote Freud. True, many attacks on Freud's ideas still appeared in medical journals, especially in Vienna, where his theories never won complete approval. Nevertheless, as a person, the professor had become a towering figure, admired and respected from Paris to Tokyo and from London to Moscow.

A French psychiatrist summed it all up when he said, "Have we ever known a psychologist, a philospher or a physician to attain such a height of fame in his lifetime? . . . Psychology, pathological medicine, literature can no longer dispense with him; the salons know no other conversation; there is no dinner party at which his name does not turn up during the dessert."

As Freud's fame spread, new waves of followers joined the psychoanalytic movement. Many, such as Princess Marie Bonaparte, began as skeptical patients and ended up as devoted disciples.

The Princess first came to see Freud in 1924, after the death of her father. Among her father's papers she had discovered a series of notebooks containing childish poems, stories, and fantasies. She was told that she had written the notebooks between the ages of seven and ten, but she had no conscious memory of having done so. To find out more about the meaning of the notebooks and about her own past, the Princess came to Vienna to be psychoanalyzed by Freud.

After only three weeks of psychoanalysis, and just by interpreting the Princess' dreams, Freud was able to describe to her early events of her own childhood that she could not remember at all. Those events, Freud explained, had influenced the content of her notebooks and had affected much of her later thought and behavior.

Astounded that the professor could "see" her past so clearly while she had no recollection of the occurrences he described, the Princess decided to check on Freud. She sought out an old groom who had served her family for many years and had helped care for her as a child. Over and over she questioned him, urging him to remember as much as he could about the past and to be completely honest with her. When the old man confirmed Freud's description of early events in the Princess' life exactly as the professor had portrayed them, she was overwhelmed. After that she visited Freud for several months a year, undergoing psychoanalysis and studying his theories and principles. She remained dedicated to Freud throughout her life, going out of her way to help him and his family whenever she could.

The Princess' devotion was typical of other new admirers who came from many parts of the world to seek Freud's help. But while Europeans were discovering Freud for the first time, it was in the United States, where he had been accepted years before, that his popularity reached its greatest heights. From there he now received a series of unusual, if doubtful, tributes.

The first came in 1924. A scandalous crime had rocked Chicago and hit the front pages of the newspapers in the United States. Two wealthy young men, Loeb and Leopold, had murdered a little boy for no apparent reason except their desire to commit a "perfect murder." During their much publicized trial, Colonel McCormick, owner of the *Chicago Tribune*, offered Freud $25,000 to come to Chicago and give his opinion of the prisoners. A rival newspaper owner, William Randolph Hearst, went a step further. He offered Freud any amount the psychoanalyst would name to travel to the United States and analyze the two youths. Hearing that Freud's health was poor, he even proposed chartering a special ship so that the professor could travel in privacy and comfort. Such obvious publicity stunts on the part of the newspapers annoyed Freud, and he turned down both publishers' invitations.

Freud found the next request from America more amusing. Samuel Goldwyn, the Hollywood director, was planning a lavish motion picture about famous love stories in history. What greater authority could he find on love and sex, he reasoned, than Sigmund Freud? In 1925, quite confident that the professor could not afford to turn down such a magnificent sum of money, Goldwyn offered Freud $100,000 to cooperate with him in making the film. To his amazement, Freud not only rejected the offer, but even refused to meet with Goldwyn to discuss it. Later an American friend reported that Freud's refusal to see the famous Goldwyn had caused as much of a sensation in the United States as his *Interpretation of Dreams* had in Vienna years before.

For all the flattery and adulation Freud received, his new fame had little more effect on him than had the earlier insults. In a modest autobiography that he published in 1925 he barely mentioned the setbacks he had suffered or the great personal triumphs he was now achieving. He merely described his theories and stated facts of his own life that had some bearing on psychoanalysis. He ended the book on a note of hope, but one that showed he was not completely convinced by his sudden popularity.

"Looking back, then, over the patchwork of my life's labours," he wrote, "I can say that I have made many beginnings and thrown out many suggestions. Something will come of them in the future, though I cannot myself tell whether it will be much or little. I can, however, express a hope that I have opened up a pathway for an important advance in our knowledge."

But if Freud chose to be modest, his admirers did not choose to treat him modestly. In 1926 his seventieth birthday became an occasion for hundreds of letters, visits, and gifts from all parts of the world. Among them were tributes from the Austrian writer Stefan Zweig, the French novelist Romain Rolland, and the great German scientist Albert Einstein.

Over the years many other persons with famous names in the arts and sciences came to call on Freud and to write his praises. He proudly counted among his friends one of the outstanding German writers of all time, Thomas Mann, author of *The Magic Mountain*. The British novelists Virginia Woolf and H. G. Wells also belonged to Freud's ever widening circle of admirers.

Freud was as much pleased by the respect these people had for his writing style as he was by the admiration they expressed for his theories. Mercilessly critical of his own works, he took great pleasure in being told by experts that he wrote beautifully. The praise was not easy to come by. Even in old age, Freud worked late into the night, polishing each word in his handwritten manuscripts so that it had literary merit as well as scientific value.

Because of the pains he took with his writings, Freud

valued an award he received in 1930 probably more than any other honor ever given him. That was the Goethe Prize, awarded by the Goethe Society of Germany. It was a literary prize—the highest given in Germany—and it was presented to Freud in recognition of his strong, clear prose style.

Reading the "charming letter" that announced the prize, Freud remembered that it was Goethe's essay on nature that had started him on his medical career well over fifty years earlier. His admiration for the German writer had continued to grow during all those years, and now he felt proud that he had proved worthy of a prize in his hero's name.

For the occasion, Freud wrote a speech in which he showed the relationship of psychoanalysis to Goethe's writings. Feeling too ill to deliver the speech himself, he asked Anna to read it for him at the dignified ceremony that took place at Goethe House in Frankfurt on August 28. A few days earlier a member of the Frankfurt city council had paid an official call on Freud to present him in person with the cherished certificate and the prize money that went with the award.

"This was the climax of my life as a citizen," Freud wrote about the Goethe Prize in a postscript to his autobiography, in 1935.

CHAPTER SEVENTEEN

"To Die in Freedom"

Admiration for Goethe helped blind Freud to the Nazi menace that was growing in Germany and threatening all Europe during the late 1920's and early 1930's.

A nation that had produced Goethe could not possibly go to the bad, he assured the American ambassador to Germany, William C. Bullitt, in 1930.

But then, how could Freud, or anyone else, guess that the nation that had produced Goethe could also produce horrors unequaled in the history of mankind? Even for Dr. Freud—the man who had uncovered the most shameful secrets of the human heart, the man whom nothing could shock—even for him, the monstrosities that would soon sweep Germany were beyond imagination.

For the moment, Freud, like others in Austria, chose to think as little as possible about neighboring Germany; he was too steeped in his own life and work. In 1930, the same year he won the Goethe Prize, his mother died. Her death at the age of ninety-five saddened Freud, but did not arouse the deep pain his other losses had caused him. His reaction, in fact, was almost one of relief. He had long feared that she might suffer the terrible blow of seeing him die ahead of her. "I was not allowed to die as long as she was alive," he said, "and now I may."

Freud was not yet ready to die, however. He had too much to do. He had just published another book, called *Civilization and Its Discontents*, in which he discussed the difficulties man faces in meeting the challenges of his civilization. Barely finished with that, he had embarked on the project of updating his *Introductory Lectures on Psychoanalysis* to include the new theories he had developed since 1917, when the book first appeared.

There were also his literary discussions with Albert Einstein. At the request of the League of Nations the two great thinkers each wrote a series of essays on the topic, "Why War?" Their purpose was to discuss the possibility of abolishing wars forever. Freud, the more pessimistic of the two, had little faith in the ability of men ever to change their ways. But like Einstein, he did not give up all hope that someday the people of the world would, indeed, put "an end to the waging of war."

The essays appeared in 1932. A year later they seemed outdated, almost naive. For in that year, 1933, Adolf Hitler seized power in Germany and began steering that nation and the world toward the most devastating war of them all, World War II.

Backed by his strong-arm troopers, Hitler began to rebuild Germany's military might. At the same time he vowed to "cleanse" his fatherland of its "non-Aryan" population so that it could follow a path of glory. He chose as his victims Germany's large and prosperous Jewish community.

Among the first persons to suffer from Hitler's persecutions were Germany's psychoanalysts. Many were Jewish; others had Jewish wives or had deep ties of friendship with their Jewish colleagues. One by one, these men and women began fleeing Germany to seek refuge in friendlier lands.

Those who might have hesitated learned quickly what their position was during the unforgettable evening of May 10, 1933. On that evening, German students, urged on by Nazi ministers, built a huge bonfire in Berlin and burned more than twenty thousand books considered "subversive" to the Nazi cause. Among the works destroyed were all the books on psychoanalysis that could be found in the city. Not only were many of these books written by the "Jew, Freud," but in and of themselves they were intolerable to the Nazis. What freer approach to men's minds and thoughts could there be than the theories of psychoanalysis? And what a terrible threat such freedom of thought was to Hitler's dreams of a worldwide dictatorship!

In Vienna, Freud was filled with horror at the destruction of psychoanalysis that was taking place in Germany. He no longer had any illusions about the lengths to which Goethe's homeland might go in the course of the new madness that had seized it. But he did have a stubborn faith in his own homeland. It can't happen here, was the attitude he adopted about Austria. He stuck to that attitude until it was almost too late.

For five years after Hitler's takeover in Germany Freud went about his daily life much as he always had. He wrote, saw patients, and won new awards and tributes from all parts of the world.

On his eightieth birthday, in 1936, the famous professor received so many bouquets from well-wishers that the Freud home looked like a flower shop. In his honor, too, almost two hundred writers signed a congratulatory address praising "this great man, with his unflagging energy." Thomas Mann, the main author of the tribute, delivered it in person to Freud.

Asked by a visitor how he felt in the midst of so much honor and praise, Freud quickly replied, "How a man of eighty feels is not a topic for conversation."

But how this man of eighty felt was very much a topic for conversation among Freud's family and friends. His cancer had eaten away more and more of his mouth and jaw. He suffered constant pain, and the pain was reflected in his gaunt figure and somber, sunken eyes. How could he survive if the Nazi terrorism did strike Austria? Would he ever consent to leave his country? Even if he did, could he manage a strenuous trip?

The answers came in March, 1938. The Nazis marched into Austria on March 11, destroying property, seizing citizens, and spreading fear and hatred wherever they went.

"It undeniably looks like the beginning of the end for me," Freud wrote.

In his heart of hearts the sick old man knew that he had no choice but to flee with his family, but he could not bear the idea of running away, of deserting his country in its saddest hour.

Then on March 15 came the looting of his home, when arrogant Nazi soldiers pushed their way into his house and took all the money he had in his safe. A week later the greedy invaders returned for more money, and this time they marched off with the most precious possession in the world to Freud—his beloved daughter Anna.

After a full day of questioning about her father and his followers, Anna was allowed to return home unharmed. Now there was no longer any doubt in Freud's mind that the time had come to leave Austria forever.

He would go to England. He had to. It was the only way possible to assure the safety of his family and the survival of his psychoanalytic movement. It was the only way, also, that would allow him to fulfill the one remaining wish he had: "to die in freedom."

The leave-taking was a complicated affair to arrange. First, Ernest Jones had to obtain permission from the British authorities for Freud and his family to settle in England. That done, there was the touchy matter of gaining Freud's release from the Nazis. As quickly as possible, Princess Marie Bonaparte and Anna Freud gathered thousands of dollars to pay the so-called "income tax"— actually a ransom—that the Nazis demanded before they would even consider issuing a visa to Freud. At the same time, under orders from President Franklin D. Roosevelt in the neutral United States, American ambassadors tried to impress on Nazi leaders Freud's worldwide importance. What a terrible scandal for the Nazis, they insisted, if any harm were to come to the founder of psychoanalysis.

The proceedings dragged on for months. Now committed to leaving, Freud grew more anxious every day. The Nazis had destroyed his psychoanalytic publishing house and seized the library of the Vienna Psycho-Analytical Society. Austrian psychoanalysts, like the German ones, had fled to other lands, hoping to come together again and establish a new society wherever Freud should settle.

Finally, on June 4, 1938, Freud, with his wife and daughter, prepared to leave the city that had been his home for seventy-eight years. His other children had managed to escape with their families beforehand. Sadly the old man bade farewell to his four sisters, some widowed, some unmarried, whom he was leaving behind in Vienna. He had not been able to arrange for their release at the moment, but looked forward to their joining him later on. In the meantime, he had left enough money to provide for their needs. He would never know that within a few years all four elderly women were gassed to death in Nazi concentration camps.

Settled in a bunk on the Orient Express, Freud barely closed his eyes. His mind was roaming over the long years that had led up to this moment of exile. But when the train entered France at three o'clock in the morning, he felt no regrets about leaving Vienna. He could only breathe a sigh of relief at the happy knowledge that never again would he have to see another Nazi.

There was a wheelchair waiting for Freud as he stepped off the train after the long, tiring trip, but the determined old refugee would have none of it. He was still strong enough to walk, head held high, into a free land.

The Freuds spent a pleasant day with Princess Marie

Bonaparte in Paris, then went on to London. In spite of the hardships of the past few months the methodical Freud had prepared himself well for his move by reading guidebooks and studying maps of the city. As they drove through the streets of London, he carefully pointed out each landmark to his wife and daughter.

For weeks after Freud's arrival in London, letters, telegrams, and gifts from admirers arrived daily. Newspapers carried blaring headlines about his activities, and warmhearted editorials welcomed him to his new home. Somewhat surprised by the enthusiastic reception, Freud described with childlike delight to his old friend Max Eitingon how "We have become popular in London overnight. 'We know all about you,' says the bank manager; and the chauffeur who drives Anna remarks: 'Oh, it's Dr. Freud's place.' "

The professor was not the only member of the family known to Londoners. Martha Freud, herself, seventyseven, quickly adjusted to her new environment. Just as she had during all her married life, she insisted on doing every bit of the family marketing herself. The spunky old woman soon became a familiar sight on the neighborhood streets as she moved from shop to shop, chatting gaily with storekeepers and looking after her household needs.

During their first few months in England the Freuds lived in a rented house. Then, in September, they moved to a home of their own at 20 Maresfield Gardens in the Hampstead section of London. It was a cozy brick building with a large garden where the professor spent many pleasant hours. Inside, Freud's consulting room looked much as it had in Vienna. His beloved collection of antiquities had been shipped from Vienna along with his books, and Martha saw to it that everything was arranged as neatly and comfortably as ever.

The only thing lacking for Freud was his favorite dog, Lün, who, according to British law, had to be quarantined for six months. The professor had acquired a great fondness for dogs in his old age, and now he missed his pet terribly. Whenever he could manage it, he rode to the kennels in the west of London to visit the furry Chow dog.

It did not take long for Professor Freud to settle into his adopted home and to pick up the strings of his life. For almost a year, until shortly before his death, he saw four patients every day, sent off dozens of letters, and continued his research and writing.

In August, 1938, he proudly saw his book *Moses and Monotheism* published. It was a brilliant but disturbing book that presented a psychoanalytic study of the Biblical Moses and his role in ancient Judaism. Most disturbing, because of its timing, was Freud's thesis that Moses was not a Jew at all, but an Egyptian nobleman who had rallied the ancient Israelites and taught them a new religion. Coming when it did, during a period when world Jewry was bent under the persecutions of the Nazis, Freud's denial of one of the most basic Jewish traditions hurt and angered many Jews. Even many of his staunchest followers criticized the work.

Freud, however, felt good about completing this book,

which he had begun four years before in Vienna. "The Moses is not an unworthy leave-taking," he told a visitor.

The "Moses" was, indeed, Freud's leave-taking as a writer, for it was the last book he completed. Another book he had worked on, a restatement of his theories, called *An Outline of Psychoanalysis*, breaks off suddenly in the middle of a sentence. The feeble professor, wasted away from illness and old age, could continue no further.

By the winter of 1939 the end was in sight. Every day Freud grew weaker and sicker. In spite of the torturous pain, the only drug he would agree to take was aspirin. "I prefer to think in torment than not to be able to think clearly," he declared.

The years of pain and suffering finally ended just before midnight on September 23, 1939, when, at the age of eighty-three, Freud died in his sleep. Three days later his body was cremated and his ashes placed in a Grecian urn that had been a favorite in his collection of antiquities.

Many of the famous men who had become his friends over the years attended Sigmund Freud's simple funeral service. Many other people from all walks of life and all parts of the globe mourned the great man who, during his lifetime, had opened up a new world of thought.

CHAPTER EIGHTEEN

His Genius Changed the World

In May, 1954, long after World War II had ended with the defeat of Nazism, a tablet was erected on the door of Berggasse 19 in Vienna, the home Sigmund Freud had been forced to flee. It read:

HERE LIVED AND WORKED PROFESSOR SIGMUND FREUD
IN THE YEARS 1891—1938. THE CREATOR AND
FOUNDER OF PSYCHO-ANALYSIS.

It was one of many such honors awarded Freud by the nation that had first mocked him and later turned him out. Even during his lifetime, in 1931, a similar plaque had been placed on the simple house in Freiberg where Freud was born. In 1949 a street in Vienna was named *Sigmund Freud Hof* in his memory. And in 1955, Ernest Jones presented a bronze bust of Freud to be placed in the arcaded courtyard of the University of Vienna. It was inscribed with a quotation from an ancient Greek drama: "Who divined the famous riddle and was a man most mighty."

The country that had accepted Freud as an old, dying refugee did not forget him either. There, in 1956, a tablet commemorating him was placed on the house in Maresfield Gardens, London, where he had lived and died.

The tablets, tributes, and presentations would probably have had as little importance to Freud as did most of the honors he received while he lived. But the reason for the honors—the continuing impact of his writings and theories long after his death—would have given him great satisfaction.

Freud had started on his path of glory modestly enough. His only goal at first had been to understand the causes of nervous diseases. Until his time, physicians had believed that these diseases stemmed from physical ailments. Where no physical cause could be found, the patient was accused of faking or was rejected as a "nuisance." Freud had taken his patients' complaints seriously. He had discovered that the mind, like the body, could cause illness. He had shown that emotions, rather than brain damages or bad nerves, lay at the basis of many sicknesses.

Using his discoveries, Freud had painstakingly developed his technique of psychoanalysis. It was a unique technique of self-understanding that forced patients to face the long-buried feelings and desires that had led to their mental disturbances. It proved so valuable that today many psychoanalysts still follow Freud's methods almost exactly as he set them down.

If Freud had done nothing more than discover the mental causes of nervous diseases and devise his method of psychoanalysis, his contributions to science and medicine would have been enormous. The implications of Freud's discoveries went far beyond science and medicine, however. They extended into all areas of life and knowledge—education and the arts, philosophy, religion, social studies.

Because of Freud there arose a new way of looking at man. Gone was the long-cherished notion that man acted on reason alone. Freud exposed the dark forces that govern each person from deep within himself. Never again could emotions and instincts, dreams and desires be ignored.

Because of Freud, philosophers and moralists could no longer speak of "good" people and "bad" people, of the "sane" and the "insane" as being worlds apart. Freud's discoveries showed that the difference between the normal and abnormal, between the criminal and the solid citizen, was just a matter of degree. The same forces— the pent-up impulses of the id—haunt every person. The thin line that separates the mentally healthy from the mentally ill, Freud taught us, is the will and ability to control these forces.

Because of Freud, problems concerning love and sex came to be spoken of more freely than ever before. Until Freud's time such problems were forbidden topics for discussion. Freud faced them honestly and courageously. He demonstrated that even young children experience feelings of love and hatred similar to those of adults. His writings opened the way for husbands and wives, parents and children to talk over their thoughts and questions about sexual matters without shame or fear.

Because of Freud a better understanding of children and childhood development grew up. Through his self-analysis and his case studies, Freud proved how important the earliest years of childhood are. His works led many parents, educators, and social agencies to substitute love and understanding for punishment in dealing with young people. As a result of his teachings, also, dozens of child guidance clinics have come into existence. At these clinics, trained men and women help children overcome emotional difficulties that, untreated, might plague them for life.

Because of Freud, artists and writers developed new subjects to paint and describe. Inspired by Freud's studies of dreams and the unconscious mind, they broke away from traditional topics and sought to capture man's hidden thoughts on canvas and paper. Surrealist painters such as Salvador Dali created weird canvases whose symbols and strange shapes often represent the dream world Freud had brought to light. Novelists such as Virginia Woolf and playwrights such as Eugene O'Neill delved deep into the minds of their characters to reveal the buried thoughts that dictated their actions.

And because of Freud a whole new vocabulary came into being. "Ego," "id," "superego," "repression," "Oedipus complex," "neurotic," "unconscious"—once these were technical words that Freud used in presenting his theories. Today they have become a part of everyday speech in many languages.

Freud's life was filled with controversy, and the controversy did not end after he died. He had worked in a field of unknowns. He could not prove his theories the way a physicist might. He could not measure emotions in a test tube or weigh instincts on a laboratory scale. For tools, Freud had only his own intuition and observations; for guidance, only his own will and unrelenting search for truth.

He could not help but offend. Without sentiment he examined the most cherished values of mankind—family life, childhood, love, religion. Without moralizing he unearthed the most primitive elements in man's heart and mind. Always he stated his findings bluntly, almost coldly. He never passed judgment. He never said, "This is how things should be." He said only, "This is how things are."

On the basis of his studies, thoughts, and observations, Freud drew sweeping conclusions. Some of those conclusions are still open to question today, more than a quarter of a century after his death. Did Freud place too much emphasis on sexual matters? How valid are his ideas about religion and anthropology? Must psychoanalysis be such a long, slow process?

In schools, hospitals, and mental health centers, students and professors still argue Freud's theories. The arguments no longer stem from disbelief or scorn as they did during Freud's lifetime, however. The questions are specific, the doubts limited. This particular theory or that certain technique needs further proof. But Freud himself? Who would doubt his influence? He has been accepted as one of the giants of the age. His genius changed the world.

Important Events in the Life of Sigmund Freud

1856   (May 6) Born in Freiberg, Moravia, part of the empire of Austria-Hungary.

1860   Moved to Vienna, Austria, Freud's home for seventy-eight years.

1865   At the age of nine, entered Sperl Gymnasium, an eight-year school.

1873   Began medical studies at the University of Vienna.

1876–82 Worked as a research scholar under Ernst Brücke at the Institute of Physiology.

1879–80 Served year of compulsory military training in Austro-Hungarian Army, using free time to translate a book by John Stuart Mill from English into German.

1881   At the age of twenty-five, received degree of Doctor of Medicine, after seven years of study.

1882   (June 17) Engaged to Martha Bernays of Hamburg; on July 31, entered the General Hospital of Vienna for clinical training before starting a private medical practice.

1884   Paper, *On Cocaine*, published, lauding uses of the drug cocaine. The drug was later proved harmful in many cases, but effective as an anesthetic in eye operations.

1885 Appointed a Docent at the University of Vienna, with the right to lecture to students. In October, left Vienna for Paris to study at the Salpêtrière under Jean Charcot.

1886 (September 13) Married Martha Bernays in Hamburg after four-and-a-half-year engagement.

1889 Spent a few weeks in Nancy, France, learning the technique of hypnotism used by Ambroise-August Liébault and Hippolyte Bernheim.

1891 Published first book, *Aphasia*, about speech disorders in children. In August, the Freuds moved to Berggasse 19 in Vienna, their home for the next forty-seven years.

1892–1896 Freud broke away from hypnotism and formulated the basic techniques and theories of psychoanalysis.

1895 With Joseph Breuer, Freud published *Studies in Hysteria*, using case histories to demonstrate his theories.

1897 (July) Began psychoanalysis of himself, triggered by death of his father in previous October.

1900 *The Interpretation of Dreams* published.

1902 Named Associate Professor at University of Vienna; Freud and first followers founded the Psychological Wednesday Society, later changed to the Vienna Psycho-Analytical Society.

1904 *Psychopathology of Everyday Life* published.

1905 *Three Essays on the Theory of Sexuality*, Freud's most scandalous book, published.

1908 (April 26) Meeting of the First International

Psycho-Analytical Congress in Salzburg, Germany.

1909   (September) Lectured at Clark University in Worcester, Massachusetts, Freud's only trip to the United States.

1913   *Totem and Taboo* published.

1914   *The History of the Psycho-Analytic Movement* published.

1917   *Introductory Lectures on Psychoanalysis* published.

1918   Lost all savings in post-World War I inflation.

1919   (January) Established psychoanalytical publishing house, the Internationaler Psychoanalytisher Verlag.

1923   *The Ego and the Id* published; in April, Freud underwent first of thirty-three operations for cancer of the jaw; in June, grandson, Heinz Rudolf, died of tuberculosis, leaving Freud grief-stricken.

1925   Short *Autobiography* published.

1926   (May 6) Received worldwide tributes in honor of his seventieth birthday.

1930   *Civilization and Its Discontents* published; in August, Freud received Goethe Prize, highest literary award in Germany, for his outstanding writing; mother died in September.

1932   Essays, *Why War?*, written with Albert Einstein.

1933   (May 10) Psychoanalytic books burned by Nazis in Berlin bonfire.

1936   Freud made Corresponding Member of British Royal Society in honor of eightieth birthday; also received personal tributes from Thomas Mann and other writers.

1938 (June 4) At age of eighty-two, left Vienna for London after Nazi invasion of Austria; on September 16, moved to his final home at 20 Maresfield Gardens in London; in August, *Moses and Monotheism* published.

1939 (September 23) Sigmund Freud died at the age of eighty-three.

Index